Public Choice vs. Deliberative Democracy

Dave McFaul

Public Choice vs. Deliberative Democracy

Amazon - Kindle Direct Publishing

ISBN: 9798598201695

About the Author

I started reading philosophy at the age of fifteen, and later achieved a B.A. in Philosophy and an M.A. in Political Science from the University of Calgary.

<u>Previous Books</u>

Metaethics: A Plurality of Good and Evil (2019)

A History of the Ideologies of the Welfare State with Special Reference to Canada' (2019)

The Cambridge School of the History of Political Philosophy (2020).

Contents

As Hannah Arendt said, we are most ourselves when we are *with* others rather than for or against them. Speech becomes "mere talk" when used simply as a means for deceiving the enemy or dazzling everyone with propaganda.

> Power is actualized only where word and deed have not parted company, where words are not empty and deeds not brutal, where words are not used to veil intentions but to disclose realities, and deeds are not used to violate and destroy but to establish relations and create new realities. (Arendt 1958, p.200)

An Overview of

Public Choice vs.

Deliberative Democracy

Rational Choice defines 'rationality' as a hierarchical ordering of preferences. Public Choice applies this economic rationality to voting and politics. But the deliberative democracy of Rawls and Habermas is not a market good. It is concerned with the debate leading up to a decision in the market or in politics, which can inspire us to redefine the common goods that shape our lives, perhaps reprioritizing our preferences. A market transaction is never made if one changes one's mind halfway through the purchase. But Rawls and Habermas think there are no moral facts until constructed by their procedure of deliberation. So as an alternative, I look at the eclectic epistemology of virtue realism as a means of analyzing today's culture war of misinformation. The following overview is roughly chronological.

The Neoliberal Economic Polity

Rational Choice is where 'rationality' is defined, mathematically and axiomatically by Kenneth Arrow (1951), as a complete and transitive hierarchical ordering of preferences. 'Complete' means nothing undecidable, either A>B or B>A or A=B. 'Transitive' means that if A>B and B>C then A>C. He found you cannot derive a public welfare formula from individual preferences. It would violate any of four conditions, such as individual preferences cannot be reversed in the macro. These conditions include having 'no dictator' to unilaterally tell others what they would really prefer, and 'consumer sovereignty' where the individual can have their preferences in any order they like, it doesn't matter how they got there. But the most suspicious condition is the 'independence of irrelevant alternatives' which says that whether one prefers A over B should not depend on outside facts. This is mistaken because we can never tell what is irrelevant until we have made our decision, we can never tell what may change our minds until after the fact and our preferences are infinitely refinable. Our preferences can change by what we learn from interacting with others in a group or community, perhaps reaching towards a consensus or at least a coordinated understanding. In coming to reorganize our priorities it not only matters that we are free to choose among the available alternatives, but that we can determine what options are even offered. This is the essence of the difference between economic rationality and political deliberation.

Public Choice applies economic rationality to analyzing voting and political behaviour. Anthony Downs (1957) argued parties only selfishly care about getting the most votes for themselves. They tend to consolidate into two main entities that share much of the same centrist policies most popular among voters, so there can be trivial difference between them. It is in their interest to remain vague and ambiguous forcing the voter to irrationally decide their vote on things other than the issues, such as the personality of the leader or the party's ideology. It is rational for voters to cut information costs so the marginal costs of increasing knowledge actually equal the slim marginal benefits one may get. Not everyone needs to be equally well informed, and why vote when one vote will make minor difference? However, some people naturally feel a need to contribute to the common good and make the future a better place. This is neither artificial nor forced.

Downs' marginalism was standard neoclassical economics. The next three texts, however, use the first-person strategic approach of game theory. William Riker (1962) argued an individual leader does not need to maximize votes and thereby ambiguity, in a majority decision where a leader only needs a minimal winning coalition there is not such a need. Ambiguity mixes with clarity depending on the leader's uncertainty over support on an issue. A leader can add to their supporters through side-payments, which continues until they are politically bankrupt and overplay their hand. That is, if they never question their motives enough to suspect doing the job may be more important than winning the game. This is obscured in the model by defining a leader as one who initiates policy, they want it to succeed as being their job. But, in practice this should not be all they care about.

Gordon Tullock (1965) looks at the strategies of an individual politician climbing the bureaucratic ladder. He says rational self-interest is to be career motivated and put work before leisure. A politician needs to be intelligent in making the right choices and ambitious in putting one's career first. A politician also sometimes needs to be somewhat unscrupulous such that, when forced to choose, one should further one's career before doing what's good for one's boss or organization. Tullock does not hold all politicians are hypocrites in that they consciously follow these practices, but organizations would run more smoothly if they did. He proudly calls this view Machiavellian, being inspired by him, and it is decidedly amoral.

In *The Calculus of Consent* (1962) Gordon Tullock and James Buchanan take the individual's perspective in choosing constitutions. They look at consensual positive-sum n-player games where everyone is made better off, as opposed to Riker's winner-takes-all games with decided winners and resentful losers. It is just that 'decision-making costs' are so expensive for unanimity, since each individual is needed they can hold out for more concessions. In compensation for the 'external costs' of having decisions go against one's interests or judgement, majority decisions *are* cheaper to decide. One can accept losses as long as it isn't systemic or drastic. Constitutions require unanimity, while everyday decisions may only need minimal winning coalitions. One may sidestep this dichotomy by trading votes on one issue for votes on another to help secure a desired outcome. This is called logrolling. Buchanan and Tullock scandalized prevalent opinion by saying nothing was wrong with it, it was normal politics. The better the vote-trading, the wider the range of activities that will be chosen to be public at the constitutional level. One can use the desire to reach a bipartisan consensus to stall changes one does not want by not bargaining in good faith and stonewalling. The example they use is calling for unanimity in order to stop unwanted taxation. In a three player game, any two players can gang up against the lone one left out and take all his money, so Buchanan and Tullock stipulate players are not allowed to gang up and press redistribution to the point of knocking others out of the game. One, therefore, has to consider the needs of other individuals in the community.

The Deliberative Alternative

The communitarian nature of political deliberation contrasts with the methodological individualism of economics. We can see community at work when I comment on the weather and take it from being true for each of us separately to making it a matter for us in common. A dialogue is an action shared between us in which we both participate together.

xvi

Through dialogue with others we can come to redefine our goals and revise our priorities. And the best way to ensure and inspire compliance with the burdens of a free society is to have a hand in creating the laws and regulations by which we live. Some people naturally feel the need to serve the greater good. Learning from participation only makes sense, however, in a public deliberation where each can think about changing one's original position as a result of the process. Unfortunately, people are often hesitant to debate politics with those who may disagree because they do not want conflict. Deliberative democracy can accommodate contrasting perspectives as we shall see.

Joseph Bessette (1980) was the first to coin the term 'deliberative democracy.' He used it to explain some seemingly counter-majoritarian conditions stipulated by Madison, such as the inability to recall a representative who needed to walk a fine line between independent thought and serving constituents. Short term passions may be unwise or unjust, the Madisonian representative should curb these impulses for a time to see if their constituents change their minds. This was not anti-democratic but deliberative sober second thought. On the other hand, Bruce Ackerman (1984) thought the Constitution carried the legitimacy put upon it by its founding moment because of the widespread participation of the citizens in determining it. This has also happened after the Civil war, and in the New Deal of the 1930s. These rare moments amend the constitution so politics can return to normal but with a different paradigm. Thus, we have deliberation depending on a strong representative, and we can have it forged by the people themselves.

Cass Sunstein (1985, 1988) further developed the term 'deliberative democracy' from Bessette. He began by defining the pluralism that underlies public choice as assuming exogenous preferences are given outside political haggling, while deliberative democracy contrarily sees preferences as the endogenous outcomes of political debate. He concedes it is a good thing deliberative institutions cannot operate without differences of opinions, but some perspectives are still better than others and this can be proven to someone who is initially skeptical. On the other hand, Bernard Manin (1985/87) agreed and complained about modeling decisions as an economic agent provided with a coherent set of preferences and given certain constraints within which they must choose the optimal solution. They are assumed to already have criteria for evaluating all possible solutions and ranking them. Instead he showed that legitimacy was *in* the debate before a decision where we can come to reflect upon and modify our views when confronted with a variety of others we had never considered before, **but** there is an open-ended quality about this because political arguments are neither necessary nor universal. They are inconclusive. Manin gives center place to argument, but he says that in the end positions are stronger or weaker as they are more or less convincing and gain more or less support. In other words, all we have is more or less pro or con attitudes which can be non-cognitive in being neither true nor false. Thus, deliberation can be justified for both the realism of Sunstein and the antirealism of Manin forming an overlapping consensus. They agree to the same policy but from competing metaphysics.

A further critique of economic rationality, and thereby public choice, is that the preferences we reveal in the market may not be the ones we truly prefer. Jon Elster (1986) showed that many people adjust their preferences to what they think they can get. While Joshua Cohen (1989) shows that people may even adjust their preferences to the assumption they are not capable of self-determination. This shows that not only do we need to be free to form preferences, we need to actually exercise our deliberative capacities in doing so. Both these restrictions affect the preferences we voice when we actually prefer something else. Through deliberation we can openly express and modify the second-order preferences we have about what preferences we would rather have.

Deliberative Democracy reaches its fullest development in the philosophical mission statements of John Rawls (1993) and Jürgen Habermas (1992/1996). They did not criticize economics so much as develop deliberation as a value in its own right. Rawls is interested in free and equal persons cooperating in a democratic society, while Habermas is concerned about a constitutional democracy with an autonomous public sphere. Rawls wants us to avoid discussing politically the comprehensive views over which we disagree. The 'principle of reciprocity' stipulates we should only put forward those arguments we sincerely think the other can accept. The goal is to reach an overlapping consensus. Habermas, on the other hand, thinks civil society and the public sphere should not be dominated by the bribes and sanctions of power and money. It is supposed to reveal problems in the lifeworld caused by these systems.

The dis-analogy between economics and political deliberation is even more sharply defined by Elizabeth

Anderson and Philip Pettit. According to Anderson (1993) democracy is different from the market because one has a voice (not just an exit) over public principles (not just unexamined wants) and no one can be excluded. In sum, democratic projects must be defined and justified in public forums to which all have access. On the other hand, bargaining is the negotiation of compromises. According to Pettit (1997) bargaining is only feasible when one has enough negotiating power to threaten the other's compliance. While debate is open to anyone who can plausibly challenge a reasoned decision and does not depend on clout. This is good because we can end up with an unjust law through procedures that are themselves just, therefore we may need open avenues to contest government decisions. In the end, deliberative democracy has different motivations from public choice. They have to be kept distinct or we can get implicated in all kinds of conflicts of interests. Integrity is putting the work and standards internal to it before any distracting temptations to put our career or wealth first. This is a moral point that can be missed by value-neutral science.

Habermas (1983) based his norms on a discourse ethics using the pragmatics of speech act theory. Speech acts found their own conditions of success. He thought being more concerned about the perlocutionary effects of bribes and threats than communicating the reasoning behind our illocutionary speech acts would be too transactional. While denying the existence of truth or norms would involve one in a performative contradiction such that they cannot be trusted to be sincere in the arguments they put forward. But Habermas and Rawls are not realists, they are constructivists. Constructivism is characteristic of Enlightenment rationalism that tries to determine the correct method by which we can construct a proper result. It relies on a decision procedure to determine if something is right or not and assumes a neutral amoral universe otherwise. To admit a moral fact would seem to put it beyond question and is therefore inherently conservative. However, Rawls modified his constructivism by turning from skeptic to agnostic because denial went beyond reasonable proof into controversial metaphysics.

But one can only refute someone who says there are no moral facts by showing them some. So I move on to virtue ethics as an eclectic realist philosophy and look at its epistemology, showing realism is not necessarily conservative. We can come to rethink our positions when we learn a new fact, which is substantive not just procedural.

Virtue Realism

We *can* have realism in moral knowledge by combining a non-natural open-ended fine-tuning in defining the natural functions/virtues contingently found practiced in society, not to mention the anthropocentric feelings that give us further insight into motives; in the same way, virtues combine what we personally think, feel, and do.

Our personal stories are embedded in the longer histories of our social traditions. According to Alasdair MacIntyre (1981) the Enlightenment's attempt to reform society, without relying on traditions specific to a people's culture, has resulted in a situation where things no longer seem to make sense or have a purpose and instrumental reason says we can't argue about our ends, only the best means to achieve them. We end up in a cultural stalemate based on non-cognitive likes and dislikes. But, *arête* (good) is a natural property insofar as the excellence of any function is to perform that function well. We can tell what we should do by knowing what our function is in a given role; we can rationally derive an 'ought' from an 'is.' Virtues are the standards of excellence appropriate to and partially definitive of a particular form of activity.

What virtues are depends on their function, but according to MacIntyre their standards and practices are capable of being systematically extended and perfected. There is a certain amount of infinity, a non-natural property, to any normative imperative in the way we can always be wrong and not know it until we correct ourselves. This is forever a necessarily open possibility. Following G. E. Moore we can say the 'good' partly involves a very real non-natural property, or ideal, that is capable of rejecting whatever natural property is put in its place. The definitions of our virtues should therefore be tentative and revisable after repeated experiences. By means of discussion we can develop our focus and discriminate more keenly, making room for the discovery of further properties that are more remote. This is open-ended, we can always learn more to refine what we think. Our feelings can even give us further insight into ourselves and others.

After many intense emotional reactions to our initial guesses, we eventually develop intuitions that shortcut the longer processes of deliberation. Life is full of ups and downs, highs and lows that affect the perceptions we have of any relevant features in a specific situation. We learn through living our life stories with all its obstacles, successes, and disappointments. For example, we all enjoy the feeling of comradery in being part of a team, but this can be good when respecting those with whom we disagree while evil hates those who are different. To exercise the required respect needed for a good democracy, we need to listen to all perspectives and be willing to change our mind as a result. Our feelings can give us invaluable insight, but we still need to test and see if our feelings do actually accommodate reality.

Instead of focusing on the nature of the proposition known, the nature of knowledge can be seen as depending more on the virtue of the knower. According to Martin Seligman and Christopher Peterson

(2004) there are certain virtues that help us gain knowledge. 'Critical thinking' is an intellectual virtue that does not jump to conclusions, considers all sides of an argument and can change one's mind if the evidence dictates. This lies within the choice and responsibility of an individual to develop over time. It should be accompanied by 'emotional intelligence,' a reliable perception of the differences in moods and motivations of others, enabling one to skillfully respond with social sensitivity and little conscious effort. Thus we have Responsibilism and Reliabilism, the two kinds of intellectual virtues distinguished by the virtue epistemology inspired by Aristotle.

These can be particularly important in a deeply divided country. According to Downs the worst case scenario is when there are opposites in a political civil war between ideological extremes with little common ground. This seems to be what we have in the US today. In this situation the virtue of a fair and open mind that is sensitive to the emotional differences between people is even more important to cultivate.

Intolerant extremism is caused and made worse internally by our selective exposure, as well as externally through a polarized us-versus-them environment. 'Motivated reasoning' is when there is a confirmation bias to favor information congruent with prior attitudes, and/or a disconfirmation bias to deny, denigrate and counter-argue evidence that does not support us. According to Downs, we cut information costs by only listening to those whose opinions we respect, whose principles of selection are most like our own, the only difference being they have more information we could use. 'Narrowcasting' is where a media outlet seeks only a small slice of the audience rather than addressing as many people as possible. This has been coupled with on-line search engines that track what gets our attention in order to find news items that would interest us, and with which we are already likely to agree. The result is we are trapped within echo chambers that repeat our own opinions to us. Added to this are apocalyptic fears about the decline of civilization that have been widely distributed because it grabs people's attention and sells loyalty to a group ideology.

Fundamentalist fideism holds we should believe on faith alone, this makes it seem like it is up to the individual to choose what's in fact true. Many people think all truth is biased and a matter of opinion. So, what if people put tribalism before the truth? What do we do about misinformation? At the most extreme we could kidnap and deprogram a brainwashed member of a cult. We could let social media police themselves, leaving terrorism as a criminal offense. We could use fines to affect the economic environment which can then indirectly modify desired behaviour. This would not deter those with deep pockets. We have to let the lawsuits work themselves out and see if that changes anything.

xxx

What we really need are more educational campaigns with plenty of public forums including people from all walks of life; legitimacy requires the participation and assent of all those affected by a decision and has to be based on inclusive considerations of all relevant reasons. Group discussions are most productive with a professional coordinator. But more informally we need, scattered throughout the population, people to take upon themselves the personal responsibility for serving and helping others by just listening and facilitating discussion. This takes more than just tolerance, it takes actually listening to others and explaining one's point of view. We have to reliably interpret the motives and feelings of others, this takes empathy and understanding which improves as we get to know them; while Miranda Fricker (2007) says we are also responsible for developing 'epistemic justice,' where we learn to compensate for the emotional prejudices that can affect us before we even think of a biased thought. We are supposed to look for where we may be wrong so we can learn and improve (see appendix). We are to test our assumptions in conversation with someone else and their alternative perspectives. As we do we can come to more fully articulate and refine what moves us, perhaps inspiring us further.

Part 1: Neoliberal Economic Polity

A) Rational and Public Choice

Michel Foucault (1979/2008) said unique to the neoliberalism inspired by Gary Becker is the way it uses economic theory to analyze noneconomic phenomena. He did not use the term 'economic imperialism' because he did not want to be polemical. The aim of this imperialism is not only to aid understanding but to critique policy in terms of efficiency in the allocation of scarce resources. A good example is Public Choice, which applies economic rationality and analysis to voting and political behaviour.

Neoliberalism is a financial conservatism that wants to take liberalism back from the progressive socialists and revive the old Manchester liberalism of the free market and free trade. They are right-wing and extremely critical of the pretentions of pure selfless service coming from politicians. Kenneth Arrow argues one cannot create a coherent general will from individual's preferences. Anthony Downs argues parties are not pure self-less servants but seek the most votes, so they move towards the center where there are the most popular policies. There may be little to differentiate them on policies, so the voter is forced to rely on irrational criteria such as ideology or the personality of the leader.

Arrow's Impossibility Theorem

Kenneth Arrow (1951) tried to derive a social welfare function to direct government expenditures, based on aggregating individual preferences that conform to conditions of market rationality. He found it couldn't be done. He thought he had undermined the communitarianism of the Idealism that inspired Marx. But the lesson to be learned from exploring Arrow's mistaken assumptions leads us directly into the alternative basis for deliberative democracy.

According to Arrow 'rationality' was a hierarchical order of preferences. It was quite concise, parsimonious, and simple with only two axioms. It had to be complete, where between any two alternatives one either preferred A to B, B to A, or was equally satisfied with A=B; nothing could be incommensurable such that we could not decide. And it had to be transitive, such that if A>B and B>C then A>C. (Anthony Downs adds two further conditions to rationality. We always choose our highest preference among the possible alternatives and we always make the same choice among the same options. Buchanan and Tullock add to rationality that one always prefers more of a good, with decreasing marginal utility.)

Arrow stipulated certain assumptions that would prove the impossibility of deriving a well-ordered social welfare function from given individual preference schedules. One assumption was that there was to be no dictator that could determine the sum of social choices unilaterally. Consumer sovereignty meant there was no limit on the universal domain of our preference ordering; we could prefer things in any order we liked. He argued for the independence of irrelevant alternatives; given any preference A>B, this should not change if another option was offered. If individuals preferred A>B, then in composite the preferences could not be reversed B>A; also a preference schedule had to be asymmetrical where if A was preferred to B, B could not be preferred to A.

The impossibility theorem follows as the result of intransitivity. For any three voters a, b, and c there could be three different priorities such that a prefers A>B and B>C, while b prefers B>C and C>A, and c prefers C>A and A>B. With these priorities the result would be intransitive, because A could be defeated two to one, B could be defeated two to one, and C could be defeated two to one. It would cycle from A>B to B>C> to C>A and back. Any point at which it would be forced to stop would be arbitrary.

Duncan Black (1958) argued intransitivity can be stopped if we simply stipulate that all preference curves have to be single peaked. Such outcomes usually favour the preferences of the median voter. Black saw there was a tendency for a democracy to fix in on two main parties. Once a party enters in on the left or the right they split the vote for that end of the spectrum. In order to win, those on the left or right must consolidate into one party again. This is further refined by Anthony Downs in saying there is a single peaked preference curve for the overall ideological tastes of voters, the two parties aim at the centrist positions most popular among voters so there may be trivial difference between them. Such an arrangement favours the median voter.

The first of Arrow's questionable assumptions is that there can be no dictator to tell everyone what to prefer. Arrow argued Idealism wrongly assumed a difference between our contingent and true will. However, we can tell the difference between an important need and an intense desire. Our ends are not incommensurable and beyond reason. We can deliberate, and some people have better understanding than others. After all we do enforce safety standards for people's better good.

The second assumption to be questioned is consumer sovereignty which means an individual can have their preferences in any order they like. Which is tantamount to saying it does not matter how the ordering is determined or how the preferences are arrived at. However, there is a difference between being a consumer and being a citizen. The consumer wants a choice over the different lifestyles given as options. The citizen wants a voice in determining which options are offered. This is the essence of the difference between deliberation and the assumptions of economic rationality.

Most importantly, the assumption that irrelevant alternatives are independent is to be held especially suspect. Arrow had an experience where he was the primary candidate to win an academic prize but one of the other candidates died and the reward was given to someone else. However, we cannot tell beforehand what might be found relevant during deliberation. Any moral rule is only a general rule of thumb because any added information could lead us to re-evaluate the ideal. The only way past decisions could determine future ones is the impossible and impractical assumption that we have already completely thought out all our alternatives. It would have to be impossible for new information to make a difference in our priorities or to what we really want when fully informed. This cannot be determined beforehand. This is very important and we will continue to refer to the open-endedness of normative concepts.

The goods in our practices can be systematically and indefinitely extended. When G. E. Moore says that after defining the Good as X, we can still validly ask whether X is actually 'good.' This points not toward another world, but to the element of infinity in all normative concepts. Infinity itself is a non-natural property that does not imply another world. That we can always improve and get better remains forever an open possibility that can never be foreclosed. It is a necessary possibility; the function of everything trying to improve itself. The ideas that the good is either a natural or non-natural property can be reconciled by putting a natural value in the place of the good while recognizing that this is only tentative and not completely adequate. We can name any natural good and cross it out with a big X to signify that it is only a best approximation for now, since it can always be trumped by an over-riding consideration in the future. (Heidegger called this 'putting under erasure.') This can't be ruled out, and points towards the infinite perfection of the Good. It points towards progress; each new generation inevitably has its own criticisms of the previous ones, possibly promoting values the others didn't see.

Johnathon Dancy in *Ethics without Principles* (2004) also suggests normativity is itself a 'non-natural' property, without postulating the reality of another Platonic world

(Dancy, 2006). Dancy's moral particularism holds that a detail of any situation can always disqualify what at best can only be a 'rule of thumb;' something generally true but not universally or necessarily so. I would say that if infinity is a non-natural property, then the fact that something can always be trumped by added information relevant for the evaluation of any good would in modal terms be an endlessly open or necessary possibility. There is no need for another world, just infinity. However, Dancy's view can undermine any attempt at a normative ethical theory because there can always be innumerable exceptions. Particularism has been called an anti-theory. But it can also mean that since normative terms are a non-natural open series, our grasp of them is infinitely perfectible, possibly inspiring us to do more than we thought we could. Any time we gain some surprising new insight we may have to redefine our goods, which in turn can cause us to reorganize our priorities.

Anthony Downs

In *An Economic Theory of Democracy* (1957) Downs models political rationality on egoism. The purpose of any party is to be elected or re-elected. A party is a loose coalition who cooperate to get some of them elected, though they may disagree on policies. This results in power struggles that form a hodgepodge of compromises rather than a single rational decision-making entity. However, they are united in wanting to get elected. Downs gleefully gloated that politicians were not pure public servants but wanted to win elections for the sake of private interests like income, power, and prestige. They pursue popular policies in pursuing their individual incentives. In the end, the government does not care about what is best for the people, only what can get them the most votes. The government in office will spend to get the most votes until this equals the votes lost through financing such as raising taxes. Constituents are left to choose every few years among the parties the elites have to offer for who will rule us.

To maximize votes, parties try to be everything to everyone – a catch-all party. This means they are so vague and ambiguous in their promises the voter may not really know on what policies they are voting. It is rational for a party to create irrationality in the voters, by getting them to vote on some other basis than the issues, such as the personality of the leader. Because the parties will tend to adopt similar policies, there may be little to really differentiate them except vague ambiguous ideologies.

The economic purpose of voting is to vote for the party which will give one more benefits than any other. A voter has to choose among the few parties the elites have to offer. A citizen will vote for the party he expects will give him the greater benefits during the next election cycle, based on past behaviour. We compare the behaviour of the incumbent with a speculated stream of utility expected from the opposition if they had been in

office, or one's image of an ideal party in a 'good society.'
This would be qualified by the trend one saw of the
incumbent getting better or worse. If a party gets re-
elected then the vote is for 'no change,' if the opposition
gets elected then the vote is for 'change.' If there was no
expected difference the voter will abstain. Voters cut
down the costs of obtaining information by always voting
the same way or abstaining. Only those who are uncertain
are open to be influenced.

Downs admits that in reality people are not always
selfish, even in politics. But then he uses it as a basic
economic assumption to determine and predict rational
behaviour anyway. Some people are just more active in
civic affairs, joining voluntary associations, donating time
and money to social or environmental causes, or even take
part in protesting because they feel the need to make the
world a better place for future generations. Because of the
discipline's prevalent assumption of self-interest,

economists have been empirically shown to be more selfish.

B) Game Theory Strategies

The next three texts use the first-person strategic approach of game theory rather than Arrow's axiomatic set theory or Downs' neoclassical marginalism. William Riker argues that in order to form a minimal winning coalition in a winner-takes-all situation a leader must offer side-payments to followers for their support, which continues until the leader is politically bankrupt and this is the primary cause of disequilibrium. Gordon Tullock created some Machiavellian strategies for a single politician climbing the bureaucratic ladder. In combination with James Buchanan they argued that with progressive taxation where taxes discriminate to pay for benefits for everyone, there will always be too much public action because any particular voter can end up paying no cost for some marginal benefits, especially with redistribution.

William Riker

In *The Theory of Political Coalitions* (1963) William H. Riker argued against Downs' idea that parties try to maximize votes, by saying all that is needed is the minimal number estimated to win. With a minimal winning number there is less need for compromise or to cloud the issues and fewer to divide the political spoils. The need for numbers and ambiguity goes up when parties do not know the preferences and loyalty of voters or the impact/weight they may add. There will be a combination of vagueness and clarity depending on the leader's uncertainty over support for specific issues. Because Riker defines rationality as wanting to win, ideology is only a tool to help the politically rational leader develop winning coalitions, not a deeply felt belief for which a leader selflessly struggles. However, when a leader changes ideologies this can cause problems for those who believed in the original position. There is a risk one may alienate one's original followers in trying to win new ones.

Downs used marginalist economics while Riker used game theory. For Downs the government in office will spend to get the most votes until this equals the votes lost through financing such as raising taxes, while voters seek information until marginal return equals marginal cost with the assumption of decreasing returns from the knowledge sought and the increasing costs of obtaining even more. For Riker politics, even more than the economy where supply mechanistically meets demand, is a matter of forming a conscious strategy in an environment where others are competitively and strategically responding to you, as in game theory.

For Downs politicians are primarily office-seekers. For Riker politicians are policy makers allocating resources and trying to minimize the number of claimants. Downs's politicians only care about winning and do not concern themselves with the policy or concessions they must make to win. Maximizing votes is costly. For Riker, a leader cannot and would not want to pay everyone, this in turn creates losers and opposition. Scarcity in politics is the satisfaction of one interest at the expense of another. In a zero-sum game one person gains what another loses so both always equal 1. In a zero-sum, winner takes all, game there is a limit such that no player is eliminated because they would rather resign than hope to win tomorrow.

According to Riker, just as there are winners and losers, there are leaders and followers. Some people simply have more weight (influence, power, significance) than others. Their role is to be leaders who need followers. Coalition building begins when a leader initiates a 'proto-coalition' in a process towards gathering enough followers to win the majority on a decision on a particular issue. A 'coalition' is at the end of the process of people moving in and out of a proto-coalition until at the point when a decision is made. One can either win or lose, or be blocked. After a coalition is winning no one can join or resign. With winners and losers and a rational preference for minimal winning coalitions, a winning coalition for one decision implies something much like it will win on the next. Individuals eventually gather into proto-coalitions until there are left two giant parties and no one can move. The two party system institutionally stabilizes the model by blocking each other.

When the original followers, who were inspired just by the leader's rhetoric and vision, are not enough to win a victory, coalitions must be expanded through side-payments. Side-payments encourage a winning coalition on one decision to continue onto others, thereby also institutionally stabilizing the system internally. The accumulation of physical force for one decision is readily available for another. Future policy and payoffs expect some permanence. Charisma takes a life time, not lost by a single decision alone.

There are five kinds of side-payments.

1. The threat of reprisal. Where there is tight party discipline a leader can threaten expulsion to a

rebellious member or a loss of office. Another example is when opposition to a bill is rhetorically portrayed in such a way as to provoke popular disapproval. As when criticisms of extending social security are portrayed as being against social security itself. Or when McCarthy accused complaints about him of being unpatriotic.

2. Money may be able to measure some valuable items. But in democracies selling votes for money is frowned upon, while in other areas of society it is neutral. Prestige may be intangible, but simple offices have themselves a value of an annual income times the number of years held. Civil service reformers also objected to patronage.

3. Promises on policy. A leader begins by attracting followers to his original proposal by the force of his persuasion. If that is not enough to win, he must attract more followers. By promising amendments,

a leader risks alienating his original followers to attract new ones.

4. Future decisions. A leader on one decision has more weight when they can play that role more often. By promising to modify support for a future decision a leader can add followers without amending present legislation. A leader on one issue may negotiate to be a follower for another leader on their issue, in turn for their support on the current decision. This is called log-rolling.

5. Some people get emotional satisfaction from following those they see as having a more-than-human instinct for right action. Anything such a leader proposes is right and good simply because *they* have suggested it. Any action, proposal, decision is its own reward because the beloved leader has initiated it.

There are three ways these side-payments are paid for.

1. 'Profits' are the gains from the decision at hand. Patronage and promises on policy content when the result of the present decision. These may seem costless, but the cost is the loss of freedom for a leader's actions. A job given to one cannot be given to another; modifying a bill one can lose the vision and lose followers; following a particular policy can alienate more than attracts. Costs cannot exceed profits. While we cannot numerically measure the objective value of a win, we can assume there will be enough to satisfy the partners without suggesting the sum of their utility is exactly equal to the objective value of the win.

2. 'Working capital' is the expenditure of present skills and possessions. Expending energy on bargaining and planning, promises on future decisions, or payments of jobs and money now in the leader's possession. These are laid out before a decision and cannot be recouped if the coalition

fails. How is a leader to measure and compare energy, money, and future decisions? All that can be said is at some point the leader will decide he has paid out all that winning is worth to him.

3. 'Fixed Assets' is where the leader stakes his whole career and life on the decision. They must win on every such decision. A threat that is not backed up will no longer threaten. Charisma that fails reveals one as a fraud. Love tainted with self-interest or indifference will be lost forever. Individual payments are genuine costs but incalculable. In payments out of fixed assets no limit can be calculated.

Because these costs are incommensurate a leader can easily miscalculate payments, causing disequilibrium. Overpayment will exhaust the leader's capacity to pay. Underpayment will lead to the disillusionment and desertion of followers.

Miscalculation is increased when one incorporates payments to the leaders. There are three pay-offs for leaders.

1. Power is the ability to get someone to do something they wouldn't otherwise do. This can instrumentally support a change in policy or victory in a conflict. Or it can be valued for its own sake.

2. Prestige. Leaders don't get emotional satisfaction from following but from being followed. Leaders may be rewarded by the sense of accomplishing a mission, or they enjoy veneration and deference. A sense of mission can help with self-doubt and low esteem.

3. Continuation. A leader who doesn't rely on threats or love may become a follower with little problem. For those who do so rely such a prospect is devastating and the aim is to keep it going. The tyrant wants to avoid retribution. If a leader's wealth is the result of his office to lose it is to lose

his fortune. To lead by love one incurs so many obligations he cannot stop and let them down. He mixes his life with theirs until he has no independent existence. He is *their* spokesman, agent, or leader and after long enough *their* life is his life, so that to cease to lead is to cease to truly live.

The significance of these pay-offs are two fold.

1. These three payments cannot be paid out of the contingent profits of the decision itself. The payment lies in winning not in what is won. A leader interested in only these three rewards can leave all the objective winnings to the followers. Those who want only power, prestige, and continuance have an advantage over those who try to hold some profit for themselves.

2. The model favours those who want to win for its own sake, there is a tendency to over-spend on victory, which uses up the leader's resources.

Because a leader's and follower's rewards cannot be cashed out in the same currency, keeping leadership going can easily be more expensive than all that is objectively won in all the victories. Leaders may pay out more than the victory is worth. Those only intent on the three rewards will promise not only all the spoils of victory but payments out of working capital and fixed assets also. This uses up those assets that ensure a leader's continuance. A leader may use up all their patronage for some trivial issue only to have nothing left to win a more important one. Side-payments can be made until the leader is eventually bankrupt and this in turn will change the weight of everything in the system. This constant pursuit of always more is the primary cause of disequilibrium.

Winning is everything for the rational politician, more so than what is won. The moral of the story in the economic metaphor of portraying politics as a matter of making side-payments to create a minimal winning coalition in a zero-sum game, is that the leadership pay-offs from politics feed the insatiable greed and vice of the political leader until his waste leads to his downfall. This is definitely a neoliberal critique of politics. Neoliberalism is a financial conservatism that wants to take liberalism back from the progressive socialists and revive the old Manchester liberalism of free trade and the free market. There is no sense that the politician may learn serving the public good can be more satisfying than obtaining pay-offs without subjecting them to long-term scrutiny.

Gordon Tullock's Bureaucracy

The value of ethics for economically analyzing politics has been sharply criticized by Gordon Tullock in *The Politics of Bureaucracy* (1965). He says that sometimes what's good for the organization and being rewarded can diverge, it is rational to choose our self-interest. Tullock uses empathy rather than mathematics to discuss interpersonal connections and strategies for the individual politician climbing the bureaucratic ladder. He defines politics as relations between superiors and subordinates in a hierarchy. Hierarchies are pyramids. This is different from economics where the transaction is between equals. The typical government employee can only obtain promotion through pleasing his superiors. 'Merit' is when advancement is the result of conscious selection by somebody in terms of characteristics thought desirable. It functions much the same way regardless of the criteria used. There are numerous situations where one may rise, remain the same, or fall. Rising is obtaining a good assignment, earning the confidence of superiors, or getting a good name around the office. Those who lose rank are kept playing with the hope they may rise again. Someone who is 'ambitious' will put career first before leisure and rise to the top. 'Intelligence,' as revealed by behaviour, is the ability to make correct decisions. If someone normally doesn't or can't make up their mind, they will lose to someone who can. Decisions are intelligent when they advance one's career.

There is no necessary conflict between what is good for the individual and what is good for the organization. Efficient management should seek to minimize such choices, so those who would put the organization first do not have to sacrifice their ideals. Those who make it to the top, however, tend to care more for themselves than the objectives of the organization. The immoral politician possesses an advantage in having a wider range of choices. Many well-adjusted politicians may not even be aware of conflicts of interests. It is not always easy to tell the difference between what is good for us and what is good for the organization. For many it is the reason they don't enter politics. Creating a good feeling of mutual confidence may allow the unscrupulous to get rewarded for behaviour that does not benefit the organization. If enough people catch onto this it can lower morale, plus the chief will hear about it. It is best to hide and pretend to be honest. Superiors do not wholly trust subordinates anyway. They ask to see the original documents, talk to other people and cross-examine employees. Superiors will do summersaults to reduce their dependence.

"The successful politician will be the one who chooses the most advantageous courses of action, not those courses which are, by some external moral code, the most righteous." (Tullock 1965, p.127) Politicians are utility maximizers that are intelligent, ambitious, and unscrupulous. Those who rise to the top will be the most rational. According to instrumental reason, only the individual can judge what they like. An outsider cannot judge the rationality of their choice. We can only judge the best means to given ends. Those who make the fewest mistakes rise to the top. Rational self-interest is to be 'career motivated.' The idealist may want to rise to the top because of all the good they can do, but when they get there they may no longer be so sure what is good. Many politicians rationalize their actions in terms of the greater good, but whether true or not we can normally treat them *as if* they are selfish. Politics is thought to be morally suspect; most have to lie, distort, cut corners, or backstab. Tullock says he is trying to understand humans and the best way they can cooperate. Taking them as they are, we save ourselves a lot of trouble and avoid judging them defective.

There are many factors that can lead to promotion. Culture is largely unconscious; people generally don't realize there are alternatives. The rational politician must conform to the cultural image of a "proper" organizational man. They must be a personality salesman exuding honesty, simplicity and intelligence. The ethics inside an organization may be different from outside, but promises must be binding and one must be loyal. Violating the internal code of the organization will end chances of promotion, if they get caught. A Politician must make it clear they think their group or organization is the best, and if moved drop their former attitude in favour of the new group. Internally peers are rivals, but they consider those who work for another sovereign to be enemies and obstacles to their group, though they may not hold this against any particular individual by themselves. Organizations and subgroups may have distinct personality types to which the politician must conform. One must study the prevalent personality type more likely to be at the top. Someone who has rigid characteristics will be stopped somewhere on the promotion ladder. People also tend to get promoted for sound judgement rather than expertise, and sometimes a good reputation can be more important for promotion than formal efficiency evaluations.

Tullock's strategy goes as follows. 'Sovereigns' are those who can punish or reward the individual politician, the ones they have to please. They are the most important part of the politician's world and it is worth studying what they will or will not reward. There may arise a conflict between what the sovereign will reward and what the politician would really prefer. However, there is a limit to what a sovereign knows. A politician may misrepresent the facts through choosing what facts are presented to control the sovereign's decision in a way that favours the politician. "The politician confronted with the choice must take two variables into account, the deviation between what he really wants and what the sovereign will reward, and the probability that the sovereign will be aware of his action." (Tullock 1965. P.71) The object is to take the path that will be rewarded, regardless of the subjective attitude of the sovereign. But pleasing the sovereign is only instrumental to what the politician really wants.

If the expert's career depends on pleasing his sovereign, they will have to consider what is the intelligence of the sovereign and what they know, because it is more important to appear right than to actually be so. Generally, they will have to adjust to the dullard's ideas or get out. The politician searches for policies that can be readily and plausibly explained to the less well informed sovereign rather than explain all the information needed for the best decision for the sovereign. The politician will not advocate policies that are too complex or deep. A sovereign does not have time to be educated by all the details, and the next promotion is likely to go to the one who can make correct decisions. The politician will not be rewarded, however, if the policy fails. Yet, they're only one of many influences affecting an outcome. A "correct" decision can be followed by a poor result.

The sovereign has two weaknesses.

1. Straight and open flattery often works, but someone with skill may not have to say a word to flatter the sovereign and make them feel their words are appreciated. Some like to argue. The politician will have to find out what company the sovereign finds pleasant. But, someone who is charming and inefficient is as little likely to get promoted as an efficient boor. One must strike a balance between flattery and performance. In a

multiple sovereign situation, a supervisor will use flattery to get to climb the bureaucratic ladder, but will not allow it to be used on them.

2. The subordinate may not be sure what the sovereign wants. Whether the sovereign doesn't really know, or don't want to make up their mind, to take action without asking his superior may meet with disapproval. But to ask can threaten one's career. The sovereign has limited time which is why the politician is there. It can also seem like the subordinate is questioning the superior's judgment, or maybe their just too stupid. Curiosity only leads to quarrels with superiors and a bad conscience, so organization men may cut themselves off from external reality.

The multiple sovereign is when the individual is confronted with several superiors who do not act as a group but individuals. It is the most common of administrative hierarchies especially in the lower ranks. In such a situation not only does one have a superior but they have a superior. Sometimes one must support one's superior against their superiors, sometimes one must go behind their back to get ahead. Knowing that one's boss talks to one's subordinates keeps an official in line, because they know they can be replaced by the subordinate. A sovereign knows the politician can switch loyalties to another. So they are more likely to reward and there is not as much pressure to loyally defer to them. There are three moves open to the aspiring politician.

1. The politician may try to improve their standing with their present sovereign.
2. The politician may to help his sovereign advance for the politician's benefit. The sovereign must be willing and able to reward the politician. This may be an implicit bargain, or the sovereign will promote the subordinate to a position of higher responsibility because they have confidence in the subordinate.

3. He may switch his allegiance. This should not be done too often. It is good to get a reputation for sticking by sovereign even in times of trouble. The politician should make the sovereign aware that though the politician is loyal they will move if they are not treated right.

Peers are equals close enough to participate in the politician's power struggles. They are the main rivals or those with which he most comes into contact. There is a hierarchy of favours, the knowledge of which and the attempts to modify dominate the plans of peers. The wise and ambitious politician must both please the sovereign and undermine the same attempts by the others. But tattling can bring disfavour. Usually one say "I don't tell tales but ..." and then carries on. The sovereign knowing his control is improved by having each tell on the other. One can arrange the sovereign to eavesdrop on a conversation, or telling a rival that the boss already knows about something so they tell on themselves. One could get the sovereign to take an interest in a field where the weaknesses of a rival can be discovered. Or, get two rivals into a conflict that will discredit them both to one's advantage. The peers are more likely to know the vices of the politicians and they may use personal details to discredit him. He must appear to both his peers and the sovereign that he is carrying out the sovereign's will. A politician must appear reliable. If he doesn't any rumor can ruin him.

Tullock says his analysis does not suggest politicians are hypocrites in that they consciously follow these practices, but organizations would run more smoothly being more rational and predictable if they did. One can call this view Machiavellian. The ambition of furthering one's career before anything else is never questioned. Perhaps we could actually wise up?

The Calculus of Consent

Instrumental reason, where our ends are beyond arbitration and we can only rationally determine the best means to those ends such as success, is part of the Enlightenment project to reform our inherited institutions in accordance with the best science. For conservative discourse to be powerful, it has to appear homogenous, universal, timeless, value neutral, impersonal, disinterested – objective. One of the best ways to do this is to rely on context free mathematics that can appear to have policy implications.

"With the philosophers of the Enlightenment we share a faith that man can rationally organize his society." (Buchanan and Tullock 1962, 308). Part of the Enlightenment project is an assumption of atomism and the individualism prevalent in economics. Gordon Tullock and James Buchanan in *The Calculus of Consent: Logical Foundations of Constitutional Democracy* (1962) argue the only way to evaluate constitutions and laws is by their effects on the individual. Basing their analysis only on rational self-interest they show that individuals will choose a constitutional democracy. Individuals are utility maximizers with different preferences; people seek different things from the political process. This seems to follow Downs' egoism, however, it is not that actors are selfish rather than altruistic, but they have different aims and purposes that can conflict, and this will not disappear when fully informed. Downs concentrates on the behaviour of political parties to attract voters, while Buchanan and Tullock look at voting and collective action from the perspective of the individual agent choosing a constitution. Public goods can only be defined in terms of individual evaluations, and group decisions are the results of individual choices when combined through specific decision-making rules. The State is merely the means for individuals to make social choices rather than private ones. It is therefore constructed by us and subject to altering and perfecting.

The problem with simple majority decisions, that require minimal winning coalitions, is they are usually all-or-nothing winner takes all, creating some resentful losers and opposition. Philip Pettit (1997) argues an objection to a government decision may be denied because the common interest may have to frustrate one party, or it is a minority judgement on the common interest. The disappointed may recognize people rationally differ, approve the decision process, and see it is a genuine attempt to determine the common interest. But this takes identifying with our community. Where this is absent the disappointed may not be able to view a judgement as anything but arbitrary; it was not a decision dictated by an interest they share or made by a procedure they accept. It is perhaps better to work by consensus, where we may not end up with our first choice but everyone can agree to it, rather than to vote and create exclusion with well-entrenched political oppositions. This is the problem with Riker's zero-sum winner-takes-all games.

Tullock and Buchanan use game theory to discuss cooperative games in politics. They argue political exchange is like the market in which an individual furthers their interest by providing another with something they need. The two cooperate for mutual benefit. A utility maximizer does not have to do so at the expense of others. Political collective action is therefore a positive-sum game as opposed to the power-maximizing of Riker's zero-sum game, where in an election winner takes all, which is not at all like the market.

Majority decisions save a lot in the costs of everyone trying to reach agreement where you only need a minimal winning coalition. In majority decisions, however, there are only winners or losers. And mutually conflicting interests can only come to an agreement through trade. In a single decision without side-payments this is impossible. Where a vote on one majority decision can be traded for a vote on another as in logrolling, then trade is possible. Those few who care more should be willing to compensate the many who care less for their support by trading in side-payments. Side-payments make sure the game is not zero-sum. If we cared as much as other people on a particular issue, or cared the same on all issues, trade would not happen. Losers can be reconciled by gaining support on issues they care more about that tend to be ignored by the majority who care less. This can help soften the blow from majority decision-making rules. Buchanan and Tullock admit, however, that their model has limitations.

> Our analysis of the constitution-making process has little relevance for a society that is characterized by a sharp cleavage of the population into distinguishable social classes or separate racial, religious, or ethnic groupings sufficient to encourage the formation of predictable political coalitions and in which one of these coalitions has a clearly advantageous position at the constitutional stage. (Buchanan and Tullock 1962, p.76)

Public Choice

Seeking to maximize their own utility an individual may support voluntary contracts for internalizing externalities, or use government constitutions to replace private decisions with public ones. The most principal factor for an individual choosing whether to opt for public action of either kind is costs. *External costs* are the result of another's actions over which the individual has no control. *Decision-making costs* are the costs in time and energy of participating in decisions where two or more have to agree. The individual is to minimize these *interdependence costs* when choosing whether to leave some actions to individuals, private organizations between voluntary agents, or government intervention. The *external costs function* compares the expected costs from disadvantageous decisions to the number needed for a decision. As the number needed increases expected costs will decrease. When decisions are unanimous there are no costs since any individual can veto. Net external costs fall. In the *decision-making costs function* costs increase at an increasing rate as the numbers needed increase. Decision-making costs in majority decisions, as varying percentages of the population, increase but not as rapidly as unanimity. Both falling external costs and increasing decision making costs combine to form a U shaped curve. The optimal point is the median bottom of the curve, the point of a simple majority (N/2) + 1.

'Pareto optimality' is when at least one person is made better off without making anyone else worse off, as defined by revealed preferences. If no one prefers A over B and at least one person prefers B over A then that is a Pareto improvement. If there are no Pareto improvements over B, then that is Pareto optimal. Identifying preference satisfaction with well-being leads one to the stated definition.[1] A change in the constitution is declared to be

---

[1] I would say that well-being cannot be identified with revealed preference satisfaction because sometimes we mistakenly want what is bad for us. It is assumed people want what's good for them so there is little critique of actual preferences and their formation. This is reinforced by assuming there are to be no interpersonal comparisons of utility and that instrumental rationality dictates we cannot

better when all individuals agree it furthers their interests. Unanimity will always move towards the Pareto frontier, but it will not necessarily wind up in the frontier or on the edge/line of the Pareto optimality curve. Side-payments are the only way to ensure that majority decisions are Pareto optimal where everyone is made better off. Unanimity will always be chosen first if we ignore decision-making costs.

External costs are eliminated by unanimity where every individual finds themselves in the winning party; while majority decision rules force the minority to accept actions they cannot prevent and for which they cannot claim compensation, the very definition of an externality. Property rights are never defined once and for all, they are subject to change by collective decision. Where significant damage may occur it will be in an individual's interest to

---

rationally determine our ultimate ends only the best means to those ends. There can be many Pareto solutions, not all of them acceptable. Consider a state where millions are starving. If there is no way of helping them without making someone worse off it is Pareto optimal.

hold out for unanimity so they can be protected from confiscation.

Where unanimity is required each individual is important, which gives them some bargaining power. In bargaining each tries to obtain the maximum benefits with the least for others. It is therefore strategic to bluff, hiding one's own preferences so as to obtain a higher surplus. This adds to decision-making costs, when every individual is needed they can hold out for greater concessions. Arrow prefers transitivity over unanimity, however, because the latter can keep us locked in a dysfunctional status quo, but unanimity avoids interpersonal comparisons and unanimous constitutions avoid the infinite regress of rules justifying rules.

Unanimity is most important for constitutions that set the ground rules for specific decisions, where one can accept a loss on one decision or another as long as it isn't systemic[2]. Constitutions are supposed to protect us from being exploited by a ruling class. An individual goes through a 'constitutional moment' when, to cut down decision costs, they always make the same choice according to some rule so conscious effort will only have to be expended when there is a need to deviate. There is no conflict of interests for individuals to choose rules for a game they find interesting, before they play it and find out how it will affect their winning. Since an individual will not know if they will be on the winning or losing side it is in their interest to have restraints on the exercise of legislative power and to be more inclusive in who gets to make decisions. For the same reason individuals are to decide on a constitution as a random representative of the group. This makes altruism indistinguishable from

---

[2] This model of creating a constitution doesn't work if there is a sharp cleavage in the population and one side has a clear advantage, such as in systemic racism.

selfishness, and this inspired Rawls' 'veil of ignorance' in the initial or original position of choosing a constitution:

> No one knows his place in society, his class position or social status, nor does anyone know his fortune in the distribution in of natural assets and abilities, his intelligence, strength and the like. I shall even assume that the parties do not know their conceptions of the good or their special psychological propensities. (Rawls 1971, p.12)

Decisions about constitutions, where the level is rules of the game rather than decisions made within those rules, demand more consensus than other laws. The external costs of disadvantageous decisions are eliminated by requiring unanimity. But since decision-making costs rapidly increase as more people are needed, some activities will be organized under rules requiring less-than-unanimous consent. With majority approval compromises to secure consensus become unnecessary, but consensus remains the standard ideal. If the constitutional decision is rational the costs of the less than optimal results of majority voting will be more than offset by the costs of decision-making. Costs are reduced for smaller homogenous populations that have some mobility.

Taxes raise revenue to pay for public goods. Members get differential benefits from public action, and the costs for everyone's benefits are differentially borne. Collective activity imposes some external costs even with side-payments, on anything less than unanimity. Side-payments convert all collective decisions into purely redistributive issues. What side payment cannot stop is the net transfer of real income between individuals or groups. In a three player game any two can gang up on one to take all his money. If the distribution of real income doesn't matter the most cost effect way to do something about redistribution is to do nothing. External costs are a necessary part of redistribution. In a majority decision where a discriminatory tax is imposed for a benefit to all, the individual can have a marginal benefit for no marginal cost. This would be too much from a constitutional point of view. The most expected external costs from decision-making rules is the overuse of redistribution, even with side-payments and Pareto optimality.

> By incorporating highly progressive, but nominally general, taxes with special-benefit public services in the fiscal process, the redistribution that is carried out far exceeds that which could be accomplished directly. (Buchanan and Tullock 1962, p.189)

Fearful of the costs of direct unrestricted redistribution an individual would never allow a government the power it now indirectly possesses through financing social programs. Understanding these costs, the individual is less likely to seek collective action.

How much of a public good is enough? Simple majority voting will cause an overinvestment in the public sector if Pareto criteria are used. Pareto optimality alone cannot assess the effects of purely redistributive transfers among persons. Redistribution imposes costs the Paretian cannot see. Whether or not an activity should be collectivized depends on the decision-making rules. The better the vote-trading the wider the range of activities that will be chosen to be public at the constitutional level. The constitution-maker does not directly choose the size and scope of the public sector or the allocation of resources. They choose organizational rules.

> To make normative statements concerning whether or not governments undertake 'too much' or 'too little' activity seems to be rather wasted effort unless one is prepared to suggest some possible modifications in the organizational rules. (Buchanan and Tullock 1962, p.201)

For Buchanan and Tullock there are basically two kinds of decision-making rules unanimity and majority. Unanimity has high decision-making costs; majority has high external costs. Constitution making has to be unanimous, there must be no external costs since this lays the groundwork for everything else. There can be no systemic bias. Unanimity is costly, however. The external costs of possibly distasteful majority decisions can hopefully be offset by the reduced costs of decision-making. Majority decisions can be used to reduce externalities from private behaviour, but externalities are neither a necessary nor sufficient condition for collective intervention. The costs of each action, however, remain to be determined and compared for the private sector, the public sector, or voluntary agreements to see which is less. All one can say now theoretically is there is a diminishing marginal utility of substitution between private and public goods, as well as between the different public goods.

Conclusion

It might be better to work towards consensus than to vote and create divisions between winners and losers with entrenched resentments. Tullock and Buchanan argue that consensus costs more because people will bluff and hold out for more. By their methodological individualism they assume people put self-interest before the "imaginary" common good. However, some people naturally put the common good before themselves without being forced, and we may accept decisions that go against us if we believe we were heard and considered in a fair process. The goal of consensus should not necessarily be complete agreement on everything, but to incorporate everyone's justified values in a coordinated understanding. It is not so much unanimity, but a vision capable of being indefinitely refined by the input of all.

Riker argued side payments can help increase support, but the catch is amendments can water down a policy alienating the original adherents. The alternative is logrolling, where one can gain a vote on something important to them in exchange for voting on something important to the other. According to Tullock and Buchanan vote-trading lowers the costs of reaching unanimity and the threat of redistribution, but ends up enshrining more public activities in the constitution.

The alternative to the unanimity of a constitution, with its protection, is majority decisions which have the external costs of not getting our first choice, which again we can accept as long as there is no systemic bias against us. The danger is in a three-player game any two can gang up against one to take all their money, but then the game is over since the loser will never play with them again and then everyone loses. Tullock and Buchanan argue that even side payments cannot stop such wholesale redistribution. So they postulate a restraint that everyone remains in the game. One does not have to maximize at the expense of someone else, public decisions should be a positive-sum game. To keep everyone in the game is, I say, to put the good of everyone before oneself, which is civic virtue. Civic virtue also calls upon us to be honest about the weight of our priorities and not simply bluff and hold out for more when consensus is being sought after. Buchanan and Tullock advise the rich to choose ruling by consensus to protect themselves, rather than reorganizing our interests and priorities in the light of sound reasons we may never have considered before so that we can come to agree on policy. One should not be maximizing one's own personal interests at the expense of everyone else. Everyone is supposed to honestly air their interests, opinions, and grievances in a public forum. That's deliberative democracy. The more inclusive and diverse the better for discovering pitfalls, sharpening our policies, and making much needed amendments.

Part 2: The Deliberative Alternative

Preamble

Communitarianism

Buchanan and Tullock (1962) say they take man as he scientifically is rather than morally as he should be, and draw normative implications from their value-neutral objective science. An example is stressing the importance and prevalence of logrolling, when this has been frowned upon as selling votes. Their individualism has implications. Instead of a conflict between the public interest and private interest, the public interest is simply the aggregate of private interests. The target of attack for this individualism was Idealism and Marx's analysis of classes. Class supposedly pre-exists the individual and determines their interests, having the individual sometimes act contrary to their personal interests to further the interests of the group. Against the Idealists they argued there is no 'general will' as a collective ideal independent of the decision-making process by which choices are aggregated from separate individuals with their different interests. The State is merely the means for individuals to make social choices rather than private ones. It is therefore constructed by us and subject to change and perfection. They believe in the Enlightenment project of reforming our institutions and traditions according to science.

I would say that maximizing our benefits orients us to consequences rather than who we are or want to be. We are members of groups, supporters of parties, and practitioners of beliefs. Defining groups as only aggregates of individuals with no such things as purely social goods, rational choice can support deregulation at the expense of national interests. We on the other hand can have roles, commitments, and friends which define who we are and affect what we would *want* to do. This is communitarian.

According to Charles Taylor (1995) there is a distinction between matters for me and for you, and those for us. When commenting on the fine weather to a neighbor, I can see your enjoying it as you can see that I am. You know that I know you know, etc. Each knows the other knows before anything is said. But when I comment on it I take it from being true for each of us separately to making it a matter for us in common and not just as an aggregation of monads. I open a dialogue as a common action between us in which we both participate together. Dialogue is the essence of community. Through dialogue with others we can come to revise our priorities and redefine our goals. As we learned with Arrow, normative concepts can be infinitely refined and our priorities are not pre-given and set in stone. Irreducibly social goods are those that are valued *because* they are shared, such as Quebec's French language or Canadian Medicare which is a common good for many.

Robert Paul Wolf (1968) explains we can derive affective, rational, and productive benefits from public goods. Any cultural event, holiday, or ritual of which we feel a part involves an affective sense of community. Politics is where people discuss, debate, plan, and make collective decisions on goals; how to balance competing ones, and how to achieve these. It is a rational community. To collaborate as a team in working on a common project, such as being in a band where the satisfaction is not just creating music but in doing it together, is to be a productive community.

Civic Virtue

According to the *Character Strengths and Virtues* handbook (2004) by Martin E. P. Seligman and Christopher Peterson, 'justice' is defined as "civic strengths that underlie healthy community life." (Seligman and Peterson 2004, p. 30) This incorporates fairness but can also include leadership and citizenship, another word for civic virtue. 'Citizenship' is defined as "working well as a member of a group or team; being loyal to the group; doing one's share." (Seligman and Peterson 2004, p. 30) It is the opposite of selfishness, self-centeredness, and egotism.

Virtues like kindness, persistence, self-regulation, humility, and gratitude help.

According to the handbook, people with the virtue of citizenship simply value the public interest over private self-interest. This is natural for some people, neither artificial nor forced. It is a personal need some people have to identify with a cause or sense of obligation to a common good beyond one's own. Altruism is not the basis for this since the interests of each are realized in the pursuit of a common good. Membership identity is an important motivator; they feel connected or identify with those whose welfare concerns them. There is a feeling of inclusion and mattering to others in the group. They are a team-player. They have a keen sense of duty, responsibility for the community, and can be trusted to pull their weight. They do this not because they are forced, but because they think that's what a member is supposed to do. They are resolute in refusing to act in their own interest at the expense of others and will sacrifice their immediate gratification for the longer-term interests of the group, but it is not blind obedience and can sometimes mean challenging unjust laws.

Such people are active in civic affairs, such as voting, joining voluntary associations, donating time and money to social or environmental causes, or even protesting. They want to make the world a better place for future generations. This is a need and a responsibility for those who have this virtue. "Family pride, school spirit, esprit de corps, and patriotism all feel good to the individual, sometimes overwhelmingly so." (Seligman and Peterson 2004, 357) There is a virtuous circle between social trust and civic engagement, socially responsible citizens tend to have a more optimistic view of human nature, neither alienated nor ethnocentric.

Civic Humanism

The attitude that valued political participation formed the basis for the ideology called civic humanism and the history of republican self-rule. One school of interpreting the history of political thought is the Cambridge School, or the Contextualist Approach. It has studied the intellectual history of republicanism that has valued civic virtue so much. In 1955, Hans Baron wrote *The Crisis of the Early Italian Renaissance: Civic Humanism and Republican Liberty in an Age of Classicism and Tyranny* which introduced the term 'Civic Humanism.' In 1966 the two volumes were combined into one book. Baron's historical thesis was that he could date the creation of civic humanism from the turn of the Fifteenth Century and the work of the historian Leonardo Bruni (1370-1444). Bruni argued that literature had flourished because of the republican liberty of the city-state Florence. What made for republican freedom was civic virtue, the result of free access of citizens to public offices and honours. "For where men are given the hope of achieving honor in the state, they take courage and raise themselves to a higher plane; where they are deprived of that hope, they grow idle and lose their strength." (Bruni as quoted in Baron 1966 p. 419)

Later, Quentin Skinner (1984/2002) would argue that further on in the Sixteenth Century Machiavelli (1469-1527) thought the best way to secure liberty was to have a free society not controlled by tyrants within or conquerors without. This meant a republic with plenty of public offices open to all the citizens, best served by the cardinal virtues prudence, courage, and temperance.[3]

J. G. A. Pocock (1975) explained that as far back as Aristotle a republic has meant self-rule, citizens taking turns in both ruling and being ruled. This had the

---

[3] Sometimes justice had to be compromised for the greater good; the prince could go on to do great glorious deeds to great fame, while a republic meant the people ruled themselves. It was the survival of the state that justified a seemingly amoral stance in the face of changing and unpredictable *fortuna*.

advantage of best incorporating and utilizing the wisdom of the multitude. The problem was it tended to be short lived. A demagogue or populist would bribe the people to turn against the elites and change the democracy into a tyranny. The problem becomes how to educate and induce civic virtue among the populace so they put the common good before themselves. He called this the Machiavellian Moment.

Before the Cambridge School, at the height of the Cold War, Hannah Arendt (1958) inspired by Aristotle declared that both capitalism and communism had it wrong in privileging the private economic necessities of life over the fleeting glory of free political speech and action. The agent needs to be disclosed in the public realm to have intersubjective reality; to be seen and heard by others as they are by us in a space of appearances. "The polis was supposed to multiply the occasions to win 'immortal fame,' that is, to multiply the chances for everybody to distinguish himself, to show in deed and word who he was in his unique distinctness." (Arendt 1958, p. 197) In 'The Revolutionary Tradition and its Lost Treasure' (1963) she explained that after a regime fell and before the creation of a new ruling party there would be no government. People had to spontaneously engage in self-rule with fellow citizens at the local level as equals, sending representatives to more general meetings with other regions. Citizens had to speak up at public meetings, voice their opinions and vote. She doesn't require this of all citizens, but it has to be an open opportunity for everyone. This defines civic humanism.

The Public Choice theorist Mancur Olsen (1965) said similar interests will not spontaneously organize people; personal incentives and punishments are needed to avoid freeriding. Inspired by Arendt, Charles Taylor (1995) argued that yes a modern free society does indeed demand certain burdens and disciplines from its citizens. These can't be enforced or taken over by the state as in a dictatorship. But the best way to ensure and inspire compliance is for us to have a hand in creating the laws and regulations by which we live, so we can identify with our political community.

Participatory and Deliberative Democracy

The civic virtue of citizenship or the ideology of civic humanism is exercised in participatory democracy, but this also leads to the politics of deliberation as something distinct from economic rationality. Stephen Elstub (2018) establishes the differences and synergies between participative and deliberative democracy. Participatory democracy was a reaction against the idea that citizens do not have the inclination or ability to participate in decision-making, and democracy is better off for it. Anthony Downs (1957) asked why vote when one vote is unlikely to make a difference? And, why become better informed when the payoff may not compensate one for the effort?

Deliberative Democracy

Instead of delegating responsibilities for law and policy to representatives, there should be plenty of opportunities for participation in decision-making in the workplace, community, media, and state; we learn skills through participation. Voting in elections is insufficient in the number and diversity of occasions to participate. Counting votes is based on equal rights, but this does not reveal the intensity of one's desire. Participatory democracy gives more decisional capacity to those more committed. And, Citizens should have real opportunities to actually affect collective decisions. It should not be the case that they are heard but not heeded, with genuine decision-making turning into mere manipulation.

Participatory democracy has been exceedingly vague however about what kinds of political participation are desirable and more concerned with the variety, breadth, and depth of the actual participation of citizens in deciding issues affecting their lives. In response to such vagueness, deliberative democracy emphasizes argumentative exchanges and reciprocal reason-giving. Deliberation emphasizes the debate before a vote, how the conclusion was reached and what influence minorities have had. Aggregative or majority-vote participatory democracy on the other hand does without deliberation, and sees political views or identities as being formed outside the democratic process and treats preferences as exogenously given. It cannot account for enhancing civic virtue, broadening one's views, nor for distinguishing authentic from manipulated preferences. Learning from participation makes sense only in a public deliberation where each can think about changing one's original position as a result of the process. Deliberative democracy leaves intact the usual institutions and meaning of 'democracy' when it should aim to further the political, economic, and social rights needed for more opportunities to participate in shaping public opinion.

Elstub ends by looking at what actually happens with people's participation in deliberation. Deliberation only works when people are informed; the more participating the more some will lack the needed interest and incentive. Some people reluctantly participate when corruption is excessive and their input is required to restore balance, but they'd rather sit out. Those most willing to deliberate are turned off by partisan and interest group politics, but would be more willing if the system was less corrupt. More people may be into deliberating, at least in homogenous groups, than this. Deliberating with those of different views can increase toleration, but reduces participation because people do not want conflict. "They refrain from engaging in argument or making a contribution that might destroy solidarity." (Elstub 2018, p.197) People tend not to talk politics with those they disagree, but they might want to persuade those with differing views if their opinion could influence a collectively binding decision. In the end,

> Participation is beneficial, but not essential, to the realization of deliberative norms, helping secure assent from all and the inclusion of all reasons.

Similarly, deliberation is beneficial, but not essential, to the realization of participatory norms, helping to educate citizens and combat inequality, while giving participatory democracy a more coherent focus. (Elstub 2018, p.198)

In *Beyond Adversary Democracy* (1980), Jane Mansbridge argued that our very real objective interests can affect the kind of deliberation in which one might want to participate. If everyone's interests are common or shared, then one might try to defend equal respect through a face-to-face dialogue seeking consensus. If people's interests clash, then one would want to protect everyone's interests equally through a secret ballot and majority vote. We should freely switch back and forth as needed. But deliberative democracy *is* distinct from economic rationality, as we will see.

Early Essays Defining

Deliberative Democracy

The philosopher who was most like the practitioners today and pioneered a concern over the quality of public deliberation was John Dewey in *The Public and its Problems* (1927). The following statement concisely defines the issue of 'deliberative democracy' with precision.

> Majority rule, just as majority rule, is as foolish as its critics charge it with being. But it never is *merely* majority rule. ... 'The means by which a majority comes to be a majority is the more important thing': antecedent debates, modification of views to meet the opinion of minorities. ... The essential need, in other words, is the improvement of the methods and conditions of debate, discussion and persuasion. (Dewey as quoted in Habermas 1996, p.304)

Joseph Bessette

Joseph Bessette was the first to coin the term 'deliberative democracy' in 1980. This was then taken up by Cass Sunstein in 1985 who inspired Joshua Cohen to use the term in 1989. Bessette's essay looks at the structure of the American Constitution which was strictly republican, meaning the sense of the majority should prevail. However, it also includes a bicameral legislature, an independent presidential office with a qualified veto over legislative acts, and a Supreme Court whose members hold office for life.

> Either the framers engaged in deception, employing democratic rhetoric to defend a less than democratic document, or they shared an understanding of majority rule according to which *certain* kinds of restraints on the popular will did not violate the basic principle itself. (Bessette 1980, p.162)

When a president vetoes legislation he is forced to explain why, and having some distance from constituent pressures and threats of recall would enable one to think more deeply and clearly. It is more accurate to interpret these devices as alternative ways of ensuring public accountability than efforts to thwart it. As Edmund Burke, the father of modern conservatism, said over 200 years ago "your representative owes you, not his industry only, but his judgement; and he betrays instead of serving you, if he sacrifices it to your opinion." The need to restrain popular majorities but also to effectuate majority rule can be reconciled in the framer's broad purpose of establishing a 'deliberative democracy.'

In *The Federalist* No. 10, Madison explains the role of representatives to ...

> refine and enlarge the public views by passing them through the medium of a chosen body of citizens, whose wisdom may best discern the true interest of their country and whose patriotism and love of justice will be least likely to sacrifice it to temporary or partial considerations. Under such a regulation it may well happen that the public voice,

pronounced by the representatives of the people,
will be more consonant to the public good than if
pronounced by the people themselves, convened
for the purpose. (Madison quoted in Bessette
1980, p.105)

Representatives can be expected to make better laws than
the people directly, because they are more knowledgeable
and experienced, they work in an environment that fosters
collective reasoning about common concerns, while
constituents lack the time, inclination, or setting to engage
in a similar enterprise. Bessette produced a hypothetical
test to see if our system is basically democratic. "If the
citizens possessed the same knowledge and experience as
their representatives and if they devoted the same
amount of time reasoning about the relevant information
and arguments presented in the legislative body, would
they reach fundamentally similar conclusions on public
policy issues as their representatives?" If the answer is yes,
then it is.

While the public can be immediate and spontaneous, it can at the same time be uninformed and unreflective. Deliberation takes longer to develop, resting on a fuller consideration of information and arguments. Leaders are to resist, for a time, unreflective popular sentiments that are unwise or unjust. According to *The Federalist* No. 71:

> When occasions present themselves in which the interests of the people are at variance with their inclinations, it is the duty of the persons, whom they have appointed to be the guardians of those interests to withstand the temporary delusion in order to give them time for more cool and sedate reflection. (Madison quoted in Bessette 1980, p.106)

Such checks were absolutely essential to the formation, expression, and effective political rule by informed and reasoned majority judgements.

There is a deliberative sense to the community embodied in our institutions. The citizenry would do its reasoning through their representatives, who must share the basic values and goals of their constituents. Policy must be firmly rooted in popular interests, dispositions, attitudes, and inclinations. Policy discussion throughout a campaign will help make sure this happens. There was a good reason to think those elected would bring with them into the office a sensitivity to the interests and concerns of their constituents. This is encouraged by the self-interest in the re-election of the office holder, which also discourages substantial deviation. At the Virginia Ratifying Convention Madison pronounced:

> I go on this great republican principle, that the people will have virtue and intelligence to select men of virtue and wisdom. Is there no virtue among us? If there be not, we are in a wretched situation. No theoretical checks, no form of government, can render us secure. To suppose that any form of government will secure liberty or happiness without any virtue in the people, is a chimerical idea. If there be sufficient virtue and intelligence in the community, it will be exercised

> in the selection of these men; so that we do not
> depend on their virtue, or put confidence in our
> rulers, but in the people who are to choose them.
> (Madison quoted in Sunstein 1988, p.1560-1)

The act of creating the new Constitution relied heavily on hopes for a capacity in the public, as a whole, to behave in the common interest. The question remains to be asked whether the Constitution has actually worked as intended? The deliberative sense of community is created *through* the operations of the institutions and does not exist outside in a way that can be measured and compared with governmental decisions. But there has been a remarkable openness to the framers' design which has been adaptive in responding to latest ideas well into the twentieth century such as with the New Deal in the 1930s. There is no necessary reason why this should continue indefinitely and there are three major problems for the future of deliberative democracy.

1. The American system is currently undemocratic in that moneyed corporate and business interests

have subverted the democracy for their own narrow ends.

2. Those who participate most intensely in politics are significantly more liberal or conservative than the rank and file party members. Decisions will be skewed in one direction or another depending on the party in power. Will latest trends threaten to replace majority rule with the more "enlightened" views of the right or left?

3. Electronic direct democracy would allow the people to make their own laws through initiatives and referendums without relying on elected representatives. Community-wide deliberation would accompany any referendum, but it would be profoundly influenced by slick advertising campaigns, the most immoderate voices on each side, and the passions of the moment.

Sound public policy demands more than the pursuit of private ambition. Leaders of knowledge and experience must work in a setting conducive to the collective deliberation of "the permanent and aggregate interests of the community." (Federalist No. 10) Instead, pluralism sees the outcomes of policy disputes as little more than logrolling and compromises among special interest advocates. Others reduce democracy to merely choosing our leaders every few years. But, the Constitution is not what each generation says it is, it embodies enduring principles of sound popular government.

Cass Sunstein

Sunstein was the next to use the term 'deliberative democracy.' More people are familiar with him than with Bessette. It was to counteract a particular evil. Modern constitutional doctrine has only one underlying evil. "The distribution of resources or opportunities to one group rather than another solely on the ground that those favoured have exercised the raw political power to obtain what they want" (Sunstein 1984, p. 1689), or "because those benefited have exercised the raw power to obtain government assistance." (Sunstein 1985, p.50-1) Sunstein calls these 'naked preferences.' "The Constitution requires some showing that a burden was imposed, or a benefit denied, for a reason other than the exercise of political power by the advantaged class." (Sunstein 1988, p. 1579)

According to pluralism naked preferences are rampant; interest groups invite them.

> Under the pluralist view, politics mediates the struggle among self-interested groups for scarce social resources. Only nominally deliberative, politics is a process of conflict and compromise among various social interests. Under the pluralist conception, people come to the political process with preselected interests that they seek to promote through political conflict and compromise. Preferences are not shaped through governance, but enter into the process as exogenous variables. (Sunstein 1984, p.31)

Pluralists would hold that representatives are to mechanically respond to constituent pressures. Laws are a kind of commodity subject to supply and demand leading to political equilibrium. Why shouldn't laws be bought and sold like commodities in a market? This might actually aggregate preferences more accurately. The goal is to ensure the various inputs are reflected accurately in legislation by aggregating citizen's existing preferences, taking wealth and background entitlements as given. The appeal of pluralism is in avoiding the tyranny of preference-shaping by public officials who see it as an object of collective control. Subordinating private interests to the common good can also be tyrannical. For pluralism the problem of partisan faction is when one group dominates the legislative or executive enough to subvert any bargaining and compromise by depriving other groups of the opportunity to assert their views.

The role of the judiciary for pluralists is merely to police the processes of representation so that all affected interest groups can participate. But the prohibition of naked preferences is a substantive value, not a procedure; it is not a market and the public good is not necessarily an aggregation. In the end, laws must be supported by arguments and reasons; they cannot simply be fought for, or the product of self-interested "deals." Private regarding reasons are insufficient. There must be an appeal to the broader public good. This limits what can be advocated, and while such policy justifications do not guarantee the success of public reason, they make it more likely. There is a transformative dimension to politics that informs our preferences about preferences. We need preference formation not necessarily strict implementation. For example, preferences that give rise to discrimination may be objectionable for that reason and are most likely distortions caused by unjust institutions. Existing distributions and preferences are a product of law. They are not natural, given, and beyond critical scrutiny. An absence of engagement or participation perhaps signaling a political equilibrium is not a very enticing prospect. Political activity is an important individual and collective good. The alternative to pluralism is republicanism.

The notion that government actions must be responsive to something other than private pressure is associated with the idea that politics is "not the reconciling but the transcending of the different interests of the society in the search for the single common good." Civic republicanism embodies a conception of politics in which preferences are not viewed as private and exogenous. Their selection is the object of the government process. (Sunstein 1984, p.1691)

The prerequisite of sound government was the willingness of citizens to subordinate their private interests to the general good. This is civic virtue. Preferences are to be shaped through politics. Dialogue and discussion are critical. Participation is not to be limited to voting or other simple statements of preference. Through discussion people can escape private interests and engage in the pursuit of the public good. "Debate and discussion help to reveal some values are superior to others. Denying that decisions about values are merely matters of taste, the republican view assumes that 'practical reason' can be used to settle social issues." (Sunstein 1985, p.32)

"Through the process of deliberation or debate, objectionable or distorted preferences might be revealed as such. Preferences are of course often shaped by the available opportunities and the existing allocation of power. ... People reject opportunities they perceive to be unavailable." (Sunstein 1985, p.82) The problem is corruption, the elimination of civic virtue, and the pursuit of self-interest by political actors. Faction is when some, using power to promote their own private ends, come to dominate the political process. Raw power would then supplant discussion and debate. Moral education is the best defense against the dangers of factions.

In 'Beyond the Republican Revival' (1988) Sunstein described four republican commitments.

1. Deliberative Democracy. "existing desires should be revisable in light of collective discussion and debate, bringing to bear alternative perspectives and additional information." (Sunstein 1988, p.1549) We

have the task of increasing information and opportunities.

2. Equality of political influence, if not economic equality.

3. Universalism, or agreement as a regulative ideal. It is possible to mediate different approaches to politics or different conceptions of the public good through discussion and dialogue to produce substantively correct outcomes as agreed to by political equals. The common good is to be found at the conclusion of a well functioning deliberative process, and empathy is understanding the position of those who don't agree with us.

4. Citizenship means political participation is an independent good. It is not the only good life, but there *does* need to be outlets for a citizen's control of national representatives and the opportunity for local self-determination.

Each of these is shaped by the others while also supporting them. To deliberate is to politically participate in seeking agreement, or at least coordinated understanding, among political equals.

History is an important corrective against assuming pluralist premises or invoking pre-political rights.

> Decisions about the nature and direction of a constitutional democracy cannot be made in the abstract and acontextually; they must appeal to reasons. Interpretation of the meaning of the relevant tradition is always an important method of social criticism; an understanding of inherited beliefs is an inevitable part of the project of constitutionalism. (Sunstein 1988, p.1563)

At the time of the framing of the American Constitution, the antifederalists were the closest to traditional republicanism. Only in small communities could one find and develop the unselfish devotion to the common good on which genuine freedom depends. All decisions should be made during a face-to-face deliberation and debate. Only a decentralized society would allow the homogeneity and dedication to the public good that would prevent degenerating into a clash of wills. The constitution would undermine this decentralisation. Citizens would lose control over their representatives and be deprived of the opportunity to participate so that civic virtue was undermined. Participation in government was a positive good that could offer a kind of happiness found nowhere else. Civil society should be an educator, not merely regulate private conduct. However, commerce threatened the underlying principles of the Revolution by generating ambition and greed, as well as dissolving communities. It is best to avoid large disparities in wealth, education, or power.

The Federalists, on the other hand, turned the problem of factionalism into one of corruption. The corruption that created factions, though undesirable, are the natural product of liberty and inequality in human faculties. According to Madison self-interest inevitably results from differences in natural talents and property ownership. The basic problem of government cannot be solved by education and the inculcation of virtue. For Madison, factions are more likely to be more severe in small republics, the pressures imposed by interest groups would lead to domination by factions under the guise of civic virtue. In a large one the diversity of interests would ensure that an insufficient number of people would have the common desire to oppress specific minorities. Besides, trying to route out all self-interest would itself be tyrannical. Conscious preference-shaping by the government would not promote liberty but destroy it. While antifederalists thought representation may be a necessary evil, Madison thought it was an opportunity for governance by officials devoted to a public good distinct from private interests, in an atmosphere favourable to the open-ended discussion of issues. On the other hand, the federalists' hospitable view of political stalemate and government inaction can be seen as an attempt to protect private property. Inaction preserves the status quo, but the connection is not logically necessary. The result was a hybrid of Burkean representation where elected members think for themselves and a pluralist capitulation to constituents. Representatives are neither to blindly follow constituent pressures nor deliberate in vacuum. In federalism there is an arena for local citizen self-determination, supplementing and complementing national institutions.

It has been popular to contrast the republicanism of the time with liberalism, but they both agreed on the importance of neutrality. This is not to be based on an unarticulated substantive theory that denies its status as such, or an unreflective preservation of the existing set of preferences or the existing distribution of wealth and entitlements, or an elaborate social theory created without making value choices.

> The notion seems more plausible if it is understood more modestly requiring (a) that certain considerations not be taken into account and (b) that political actors offer public-regarding

> justifications for social outcomes, or for deviations
> from ordinary norms. (Sunstein 1988, p.1568)

The equal protection clause ensures that certain reasons do not play a role in government decisions. If one person or group is to be treated differently that must be the result of a legislative deliberation. It is better to live with the problems of evidence than to strike down or uphold all actions that may or may not have an invidious purpose. The degree of constraint the requirement of consistently applying one's substantive theory implies is a controversial and tricky question, but it would be a mistake to either abandon it altogether or to completely eliminate partiality and bias. Individual and collective freedom is merely having a critical distance from our ends and being able to subject them to scrutiny. In this way liberty is collective self-determination. Rights are a product of a well-functioning deliberative process, and not pre-given. On republican grounds, however, it is not clear that neutrality among competing conceptions of the good life is always desirable, even if possible.

Anti-republicans complain that some of the central notions of republicanism ignore the persistence of differences and oppositions among social groups.

> In a large and diverse nation, there is no common good to be mediated through discussion; there is no unitary political truth; there are instead irreducibly opposed perspectives and interests. ... The problem of modern politics is emphatically not that political actors have been disabled from bringing prepolitical interests to the process. (Sunstein 1988, p.1572)

Interest group "deals" merely replicate the existing distribution of social power that is so unsatisfying. Yet anti-republicans agree with pluralists on a number of other points. Interests are exogenous and pre-political. Governmental processes are largely a matter of deals serving self-interests. It is normal and legitimate for political actors to seek goods or opportunities solely on the ground that it is in their interest to do so. There is reason to be suspicious of the state and measures that purport to reflect a unitary good. The notion of mediating conflicting goods seems like a fantasy. Individual and group autonomy are highly valued.

The Anti-republicans did not see society as a unified whole. Civil society involves all kinds of intermediate organizations between personal business and public government that mediate the relationship between the individual and the state. Sunstein agrees republicanism should be more appreciative of these and foster them. However, he adds that since these can also be a source of oppression themselves, they cannot be allowed to operate without limits. And, studying intermediate organizations does not explain what government itself should do. "Government is uniquely able to undertake a wide range of tasks, including (for example) the elimination of discrimination, the regulation of broadcasting, and the protection of the environment." (Sunstein 1988, p.1574)

In rebutting the anti-republicans, Sunstein argues that universalism does not deny the existence of different perspectives but does hold some are better than others and this claim can be vindicated through discussion with those who are initially skeptical. What is required is public-regarding justifications offered after multiple points of view have been consulted and (to the extent possible) genuinely understood. An understanding of the partiality of one's own perspective is a regulative ideal for politics. To deny universality is to give no account of the normative foundations of one's own rhetoric which depends on convincing someone through non-violent, non-coercive dialogue to agree with us as equals. Universalism does not have a desire to erase differences. Disagreement is creative and productive. It is highly congenial to and an indispensable part of the republican faith in political dialogue. Discussion and deliberation depend for their legitimacy and efficacy on the existence of conflicting views. Heterogeneity is necessary if republican systems are to work.

How do the Courts enforce the prohibition against naked preferences? The first response is to inspect with heightened scrutiny to see whether some public end was actually involved other than the exercise of raw power. However, some ends can be declared illegitimate even if they are not an exercise of raw political power. This supplements the procedural requirements of heightened scrutiny with a substantive constraint of impermissible goals. Rights on the other hand create shields of private autonomy that operate regardless of the end government is trying to achieve. With heightened scrutiny, due process and equal protection impose the minimal requirement that government action be reasonable. 'Rationality review' represents a judicial search for some public value by which to justify the measure in question.

1. There has to be a close connection between the assumed public value and the means the legislature has chosen to promote it.

2. There has to have been an exhaustive search for less restrictive alternatives.

The Administrative Procedure Act requires agencies support their decisions in terms of statutorily relevant facts. This should improve representative politics by ensuring the deliberative process is focused on those purposes and the extent to which the measures serve them. Actually identifying the true purpose served by a statute may diminish the likelihood of its enactment. Boilerplate justifications representing not the actual process of decision, but instead a necessary bow to the courts, is not an unambiguous good. Courts tend to be deferential in assuming legislative outcomes can be justified by reference to some public value, and are even willing to hypothesize legitimate ends not realistically

94

attributable to the enacting legislature. It is nearly always possible to justify an action on grounds other than the raw exercise of political power. Under a strengthened system of rational review, courts would not be as willing to hypothesize legitimate legislative purposes, and they would require a closer fit between statutory means and legitimate ends; a merely plausible connection is not enough.

Sometimes ideology has to be subject to "reasoned analysis." The Courts should be willing to examine public value justifications to see whether such were in fact rooted in or a disguise for existing relations of power. It is insufficient to invoke a plausible, even widely held conception of the public interest to impose discriminatory classifications. The public value justification has to survive critical scrutiny designed to ensure it is not itself a product of existing relations of power. Some classifications that would be unconstitutional if they were the product of an unreflective process would be upheld if they were the result of "reasoned analysis."

Sunstein admits the Courts are not well suited to their task. Ascertaining factional control involves unmanageable inquiries into legislative motivation and the drafting process. Conceptions of the common good and the desire to get re-elected are inseparably intertwined, making for constantly mixed motivations. The problem is truly intractable when dealing with a multimember decision-making body. Besides, the Courts are not Immune to ideology. It is not even clear there is such a thing as "reasoned analysis," constituting a neutral standpoint from which to assess social issues.

Sunstein believes the judiciary should be activist and correct unjustified legislation through rationality reviews. Like Madison's representatives, judges are supposed to be somewhat independent of common opinion and public pressures, concentrating only on the requirements of justice for each specific case. That's why

Supreme Court judges are appointed for life. Frank Michelman (1986), another advocate for republican jurisprudence, argues that Sunstein's rarefied position in effect removes deliberative democracy from the experience of most people. However, Bruce Ackerman offers an alternative.

Inspired by Thomas Kuhn's distinction between normal and revolutionary science, Ackerman (1984) argued that during times of normal politics the pluralist pursuit of maximizing individual interests describes the situation perfectly, but once in a while people become dissatisfied with the status quo and they get together through unconventional means to make a constitutional amendment that can change everything. This entails justification through wide-spread participation rather than by remote representatives. Michelman thought deliberation by 'we, the people' is 'jurisgenerative,' originating and establishing its own paradigm of justice.

This has only happened three times according to Ackerman: during the Revolution, after the civil war, and in the 1930s with the New Deal. These movements reformed the Constitution so normal politics could proceed again, though slightly differently according to the new paradigm. Michelman (1988) complains that while this enables self-government to be something achievable by many, it gives too much deference to the past founding moments. Ackerman's exceptional episodes of public participation should be continued through into the present in what Michelman calls 'dialogic constitutionalism;' e.g. Civil Rights were created through on-going dialogue with the experiences of the Black community and feminists. He says such …

> is a process of personal self-revision under social-dialogic stimulation. It contemplates, then, a self whose identity and freedom consist, in part, in its capacity for reflexively critical reconsideration of the ends and commitments that it already has and that make it who it is. Such a self necessarily

obtains its self-critical resources from ... beyond its own pre-critical life and experience, which is to say communicatively, by reaching for the perspectives of other and different persons. (Michelman 1988, p.1528)

The suggestion is that the pursuit of political freedom through law depends on "our" constant reach for inclusion of the other, of the hitherto excluded. (Michelman 1988, p.1529)

It challenges "the people's" self-enclosing tendency to assume their own moral completion as they now are and thus to deny themselves the plurality on which their capacity for transformative self-renewal depends. (Michelman 1988, p.1532)

For Michelman, one's objective in self-revisionist deliberating is not the exercise of civic virtue, but to promote liberty through self-government. He (1986, p.75) argues the counter-majoritarian interpretation of the Constitution is pessimistic and sees only a finite amount of sovereignty or power; as much power as we give to the Courts we deny to ourselves, because if we define freedom as being able to do as we please, then we can collide with the intentions of others to do the same. But if freedom means 'socially situated self-direction in fellowship with equally self-directing others,' then one realizes one's own freedom by confirming the freedom of others.

Bernard Manin

So much for jurisprudence and the transition from republicanism to deliberative democracy. Deliberative Democracy as an academic subject was established by three particular essays (Manin 1987, Elster 1986, Cohen 1989). These were inspired by John Rawls and Jürgen Habermas, while also critiquing and influencing them. Rawls brought out *Political Liberalism* in 1993, and Habermas' *Between Facts and Norms* was written in German in 1992 and translated in 1996. Bernard Manin drafted his essay 'On Legitimacy and Political Deliberation' in 1985, which was translated from the French in 1987.

To begin, Aristotle took deliberation to mean "the process of the formation of the will, the particular moment that precedes choice, and in which the individual ponders different solutions before settling for one of them." (Manin 1987, p.345) But for Rousseau deliberation means the choice itself, not the process that leads to the choice. It is an immediate and direct expression of the people's will. Rousseau did not favor debate. He thought that when special interests begin the general will is no longer the will of all; "contradictions and debates arise, and the best point of view is no longer accepted without disputes." (Rousseau quoted in Manin 1987, p.346) What must be excluded is rhetoric and persuasion by which some gain power over others. Rousseau's individuals are supposed to already know what they want before they decide in common in a public assembly. Any persuasion could only taint their will and suppress it. Since individual choices are completely determined, the collective decision either does or does not conform to the sum of individual decisions. There is a truth to the matter.

The requirement for unanimity, the absence of deliberation, and the predetermined wills of individuals are also to be found in Rawls *A Theory of Justice* (1971). In the original position there were no arguments among individuals because they all had the same point of view. He models the decision as an economic agent provided with a coherent set of preferences given certain constraints within which they must choose the optimal solution. They are assumed to already have criteria for evaluating all viable solutions and ranking them. The criteria are set, as is the set of solutions; the result is contained in the premises. Reflection and calculations teach one nothing about one's preferences; the procedure for forming the will loses its importance.

In the real world people never have all the needed information. It is always fragmentary and incomplete, yet we must reach a decision in time. Information at the

102

beginning which was incomplete becomes firmer through deliberation without ever becoming complete. Deliberation is a procedure for becoming better informed.

> Political decision making is by its nature a choice under uncertainty. In the process of exchanging evidence related to proposed solutions, individuals discover information they did not previously have. They learn that a given choice will have a given consequence, and if these consequences contradict the original objective they may be led to alter that objective. (Manin 1987, p.349)

When faced with an unpalatable consequence they have never considered before (the trade off between low taxes and social programs) an agent can either accept the unpalatable consequence and discover a preference they did not have at the start (preferring lower taxes to social programs) or they may not accept it and then have to revise their original choice. They may discover the opinion they held at the outset is prejudiced and decide to change it. It is unrealistic and unreasonable to assume individuals have from the start a coherent set of preferences. Initial desires are frequently in conflict, not just because different people want different things, but the individual themselves may have mixed feelings.

> In the course of deliberation and the exchange of points of view, individuals become aware of the conflicts inherent in their own desires. This leads them to modify the objectives they held at the start, to give up some of them and to tone some of them down in order to make them compatible with others, thus bringing about a conciliation or compromise. (Manin 1987, p.350)

It's not that individuals beginning deliberation don't know anything. They know they have certain preferences and some information, but these are "unsure, incomplete, often confused and opposed to one another. The process of deliberation, the confrontation of different points of view, helps to clarify information and to sharpen their own preferences." (Manin 1987, p.351) The process of the formation of the collective will does not consist in totaling up previously formed intentions or wills. These are decided in the course of deliberation. Legitimacy is the process of deliberation itself. An individual's freedom consists in being able to arrive at a decision by a process of research and comparison among various solutions. When a decision is imposed on all, it seems reasonable to give everyone the option to deliberate. Legitimate law is the result of general deliberation, not the expression of a general will.

> Everyone reasons for himself, finding arguments, and weighing them. Because the aim of the deliberative process is to broaden the participants' information and enable them to discover their own preferences, that process requires a multiplicity of points of view and/or arguments. As the individual listens to arguments formulated by others, he broadens his own point of view and becomes aware of things he had not perceived at the outset. Deliberation requires not only multiple but conflicting points of view because conflict of some sort is the essence of politics. The parties in deliberation will not be content to defend their

> own positions, but will try to refute the arguments of the positions of which they disapprove. New information emerges as each uncovers the potentially harmful consequences of the other parties' proposals. (Manin 1987, p.352)

Citizens try to persuade each other and argue, but it is not a logical proof that results in a necessary conclusion the audience cannot reject. Argument does not start from evident premises or even conventional ones. One starts by offering propositions one thinks others already accept. Also the process of linking propositions are not logically binding. The passage from one proposition to another is not strictly necessary. Therefore, they are neither true nor false but stronger or weaker as they are more or less convincing and gain more or less support.[4] No

---

[4] Manin may have deliberation based on argument and not be arbitrary, but for his metaethics he falls back on an anti-realism, usually associated with non-cognitivism, of propositions being neither true nor false, but only more or less pro or con reactions. This does not necessarily follow from the idea morals are neither universal nor necessary. They don't have to be, to be real. It could be a rule of thumb, or a Sittlichkeit - a specific community's way of life.

science can resolve moral/political conflict, but that does not mean it is arbitrary. Some values are more likely to win the approval of reasonable people. It is impossible to demonstrate their soundness, and the conclusion is not incontestable. Norms can only be more or less justified as measured by the intensity of the approval they arouse. Deliberation does not enable us to derive necessary and universally accepted truths. It also does not enable us to absolutely and incontestably refute a norm or value. A failure is not sufficient to refute a policy nor the normative principle from which it was derived. One could always argue it should have been done differently or not as much. A failure does not refute a political principle; it only creates a presumption against it. Manin holds political deliberation and science are irreducibly different. "One does not really say that the scientific community deliberates when it exchanges conjectures and refutations." (Manin 1987, p.355)

Deliberative Democracy

A diversity of points of view is essential both for individual liberty and for the rationality of the process, and an attempt is made to reconcile conflicting views wherever possible. Individuals must have a choice and the exchange of arguments allows the comparison of reasons. Anthony Downs (1957) saw the competition between parties was like that of producers facing consumers. Candidates for positions of power compete with each other for the most votes. Because they want power they are acting in their own interest. Voters may care more about the image of the leader than their programs. Not just services, but a point of view concerning the public good. Politicians must use the principles and arguments most likely to win the most agreement, universally before the full set of citizens. Each trying to show their own view is more general than the others. But universalism is not assumed at the start. It is an ideal to be aimed at. The deliberative process never results in strictly universal proposals anyway. The minority have their reasons but these have simply been less

convincing.

If a voter chooses poorly the consequences are

only apparent after a long time. The voter would change

their mind but by then it would be too late. Like

consumers they might choose those options whose effects

they can see affect them most deeply and clearly. The

issues that don't affect them may be neglected regardless

of their importance for society. Citizens have to be

persuaded because they cannot see the effects of their

decision immediately and directly themselves. The aim of

competition is to offer voters a range of solutions

according to their predetermined needs, but also to

enlighten them about their needs and weigh the options

of the different parties. Pure competition in the market

requires the maximal dispersion of forces, coalitions are

not permitted. But if the objective of conflict among

different points of view is in forming the will, we need

some diversity but not an extreme multiplicity. Political

pluralism implies a drastic reduction in the number of solutions. We cannot deliberate everything. The cost of exploring all possibilities would be enormous. Political parties enable the deliberation by all of matters already relatively determined. But it is necessary that all individuals be given a choice among different alternatives, all of which must be realistically possible.

> Because it comes at the close of a deliberative process in which everyone was able to take part, choose among several solutions, and remain free to approve or refuse the conclusions developed from the argument, the result carries legitimacy. The decision results from a process in which the minority point of view was also taken into consideration. Although the decision does not conform to all points of view, it is the result of the confrontation between them. ... A political decision is legitimate because it has been able to win the approval of the majority at the conclusion of a process of free confrontation among various points of view. ... The deliberative perspective enables us to drop the requirements of strict universality of

application or unanimity of approval. (Manin 1987, p.359)

There is no need for the untenable fiction that the majority will is the will of all or equivalent to the unanimous will. Sieyès states majority rule is simply a practical necessity, a convenient convention for a realistic principle of decision making. It is only the decision of the greatest number, nothing more. Yet this makes it possible to take the interests and opinions of minorities into account. Institutions must be set up so the majority is forced to consider the minority's view. Counterforces, checks and balances are necessary because the majority will is not the will of all. These are justified by giving a voice to minorities. The decision of the majority has to impose itself where there can be no compromises, and groups or associations offer limited protection for minority views, but when it works well the system encourages the majority to consider these views or else expect resistance. A power that faces no obstacle will have both less cause to deliberate on its decisions and less need to justify them. In a democracy, if the majority seek to simply impose their will, it would have to be intentional and deliberate. What the majority must not do is exclude anyone from voting or participating in deliberation. Nor can it suppress the fundamental liberties of freedom of conscience, of opinion, of speech, and of association. The majority cannot exclude any group because they disagree with the majority, and the majority should also not be able to eliminate the diversity of proposed solutions.

Jon Elster

In 'The Market and the Forum: Three Varieties of Political Theory' (1986/1997) Elster contrasts deliberation to market transactions, and to participatory democracy. He was critical of social choice, which is like public choice only applied to clubs, committees, and associations instead of politics. He began by arguing the preferences people choose to express may not be a good guide to what they really prefer. It is hard to defend that social choice represents the common good when everyone might prefer some other outcome than what they voiced. People may vote for only what they think they can get. This is an adaptive preference. Counter-adaptive preferences such as 'the grass is always greener' or 'forbidden fruit always tastes sweeter' baffle the rational choice theorist because they imply that if respected they could not be satisfied, yet the whole point of respecting them is to enable them to be satisfied. Consumer sovereignty is acceptable when their choice affects only themselves, but with political choice an individual can have a preference that affects different people differently. Also, the Greek polis was an open and public activity, not the isolated and private expression of preferences that occurs in buying and selling.

It has been assumed the only alternative to the aggregation of given preferences is censorship which is always wrong. But instead we can have a transformation of preferences through public and rational discussion. Rather than aggregating or filtering preferences, the political system should be set up for changing preferences through public debate.

> The input to the social choice mechanism would then not be the raw, quite possibly selfish or irrational, preferences that operate in the market, but informed and other-regarding preferences. ... When the private and idiosyncratic wants have been shaped and purged in public discussion about the public good, uniquely determined rational desires would emerge. Not optimal compromise, but unanimous agreement is the goal of politics. (Elster 1986/1997, p.11-12)

It is pragmatically impossible to argue that a given solution should be chosen just because it is good for oneself. And going through the motions of rational discussion tends to bring about the real thing.

> The conceptual impossibility of expressing selfish arguments in a debate about the public good, and the psychological difficulty of expressing other-regarding preferences without ultimately coming to acquire them, jointly bring it about that public

discussion tends to promote the common good.
(Elster 1986/1997, p.12)

This would not simply be the Pareto-optimal realization of given preferences, but the outcome of preferences that are shaped by a concern for the common good. The transformation of preferences can do no more than supplement the aggregation of preferences, however. It does not replace it.

Elster warns a little discussion can be dangerous when it makes some, but not all, align themselves with the common good. "When others act nonmorally, there may be an obligation to deviate not only from what they do, but also from the behavior that would have been optimal if adopted by everybody. ... Something like irony, eloquence or propaganda might be needed, involving less respect for the interlocutor that what would prevail in the ideal speech situation." (Elster 1986/1997, p.18) In this way Elster distances himself from Habermas while still being inspired by him. But for Habermas the ideal speech situation is really preconditions for truthful communication not an ideal towards which we should strive. They must be logically assumed if we are to engage in a mode of thought essential to rational life.

Elster also contrasts deliberative democracy with participatory democracy. The benefits of participation are by-products of political activity. Any attempts to turn them into the main purpose would make them evaporate.

Although discussion and deliberation in other contexts may be independent sources of enjoyment, the satisfaction one derives from political discussion is parasitic on decision making. Political debate is about what to do – not about what ought to be the case. It is defined by this practical purpose, not by its subject matter. (Elster 1986/1997, p.25)

Joshua Cohen

Cohen wrote 'Deliberation and Democratic Legitimacy' in 1989. By this time Cohen had read Sunstein, but not Bessette, and picked up the term deliberative democracy from him. Cohen is inspired by Rawls but not without some distance. Democratic politics involves public deliberation focused on the common good, some obvious manifest equality, and shapes the identity and interests of citizens in a way that contributes to a public conception of the common good. "There is a need to decide on an agenda, to propose alternative solutions to the problems on the agenda, supporting those solutions with reasons, and to conclude by settling on an alternative." (Cohen 1989/1997, p.73)

Since we accept the intuitive ideal of a fair system of cooperation which we want our institutions to mirror, we arrive directly at the requirement of equal liberties, rather than indirectly through a hypothetical choice of that requirement under fair conditions. We should strive to mirror the original position in our political institutions rather than as an initial choice situation in which the regulative ideal for those institutions are selected. A critic may argue that from the original position it is not clear why debate should focus on the common good, or why there must be manifest equality. The pluralist vision of bargaining with fair representation for all groups seems good enough. Cohen responds that we cannot expect outcomes that advance the common good if no one is looking for them. He argues that perhaps we should not so much seek to mirror fairness in our political arrangements, but rather mirror a system of 'ideal deliberation.' The stability of a society may require widespread allegiance to a specific conception of the good, even though its institutions can be justified without appeal to that conception. Members share a commitment to coordinating their activities within institutions that make deliberation possible according to norms arrived at through deliberation.

1. 'Ideal deliberation' is free. Members are only bound by the results of deliberation and the preconditions for that deliberation. Proposals are not constrained by the authority of prior norms or

requirements. It also assumes we can act from the results.

2. Deliberation is reasoned. Members are required to state their reasons for advancing proposals, supporting them, or criticizing them. They give reasons expecting they could settle the fate of their proposal. Proposals may be rejected because they are not defended with acceptable reasons, even though they could be.

3. The parties to a debate are formally and substantively equal. On the one hand this means public funding of political parties and restrictions on private political spending, plus a progressive income tax to limit disparities of wealth and ensure the agenda is not dominated by the interests of the wealthy. Alternatively, rules do not single out individuals. Each can put issues on the agenda, propose solutions, and offer reasons for their support or not of the proposals. Each has an equal voice in the decision. Power and resources do not shape the chances to contribute, or play an authoritative role in debate. Participants do not see themselves as bound by the existing system of rights except insofar as it establishes the

framework of free deliberation among equals. Even that is open to discussion.

4. Deliberation aims at a consensus. They must find reasons persuasive to all those who are committed to acting on the results of a free and reasoned assessment of alternatives by equals. The results of voting among those so committed is different than an aggregation that proceeds without it. Taking the commitment seriously is likely to require a willingness to revise one's understanding of one's own preferences and convictions.

"While public deliberation may be organized around appeals to the common good, is there any reason to think that even ideal deliberation would not consist in efforts to disguise personal or class advantage as the common advantage?" (Cohen 1989/1997, p.76) Members are to be committed to resolving their differences through deliberation. While my reason is good enough for me, I must find reasons to make my proposal persuasive to those who might not agree with my personal interests. This shapes motivation in two ways. The practice of presenting reasons will contribute to a commitment of using deliberative resolution for political questions. This is likely to increase the sincere representation of preferences while strategic misrepresentation declines. Secondly, it will shape the content of preferences as well. If I can offer no persuasive reasons for my proposal that may transform the preference that motivated the proposal. Aims inconsistent with deliberative agreement may tend to lose their force. Hence deliberation tends to be about common goods.

Elster talks of 'adaptive preferences' when they shift with changes in the circumstances of the agent without a deliberate contribution on their part. Cohen adds 'accomodationist preferences,' psychological adjustments to conditions of subordination in which individuals are not recognized as having the capacity for self-government. This aims at minimizing frustration. "Stoic slaves do not act autonomously when they seek to be good slaves." (Cohen 1989/1997, p.78) 'Adaptive preferences' show the importance of conditions that permit and encourage the deliberative *formation* of preferences, while 'accomodationist preferences' show the need for favorable conditions for the *exercise* of deliberative capacities. It takes reason itself to break through prejudice and self-complacency to enable us to become more autonomous.

> We seek, inter alia, to design institutions that focus political debate on the common good, that shape the identity and interests of citizens in ways that contribute to an attachment to the common good, and that provide the favorable conditions for the exercise of deliberative powers that are required for autonomy. (Cohen 1989/1997, p.79)

Rawls and Habermas do not distinguish themselves so much from Public Choice, but develop deliberative democracy positively as an ideal in its own right.

Jürgen Habermas

Popular Sovereignty as Procedure

The French Revolution

Habermas' inspiration for discursive ethics and deliberative politics began with the French Revolution. The inheritance of the French Revolution was seen as a theoretically informed realization of human rights derived from the principles of practical reason. This has lost its dramatic aura, but the liquefaction of traditions is now permanent and the norm. We still want a better future but we have lost our confidence that things can be changed by revolution. Revolution is a project that is both permanent and quotidian; a failure but also unrelinquishable.

Habermas was particularly inspired by two streams of ideology that began around the time of the French Revolution: Liberalism and Anarchism. He called for a constitutional democracy with a vibrant autonomous public sphere.

Liberalism

The German democrat Julius Frobel agreed with Rousseau that laws are required to be justified for all, while the legislature decides by majority. It is possible to combine consensus with majority rule, if the latter has an internal relation to the search for truth. Public discourse must mediate between the opinion of all and the will of the majority of representatives. A discussion provisionally closes only in order to decide. The majority decision is a conditional consensus as the minority conforms to the will of the majority. This does not mean the opinion of the minority is wrong and they must abandon their aims, but merely forego their practical application until they better establish their reasons and gain the needed votes.

A majoritarian unified will is compatible with an equality of individual wills if it reduces error on the way to a conviction. This means an elevated level of education for all and the freedom to express and campaign for theoretical opinions. Associations only influence public opinion through argument. Frobel's public is no longer a social *body* as it was for Rousseau. "It is only the medium for a multi-vocal process of opinion-formation that substitutes mutual understanding for power and rationally motivates majoritarian decisions." (Habermas 1988/1996, p.476)

Thanks to the socialists economic power became an issue that made it possible to criticize legal formalism, because substantive rights were actually unequal while being declared formally/literally equal. Habermas insisted class discrimination should not influence deliberation.

Anarchism

For Anarchists face to face contacts were supposed to be a strong enough source of intersubjective deliberation/decision-making to keep all the other institutions from congealing into set form. This anti-institutionalism was similar to the liberal's free public sphere. Discussion was power dissolving. "One no longer needs to conceive of domination-free society as an instrumental and hence prepolitical order established on the basis of contracts, that is, through the self-interested agreements of private persons oriented toward success." (Habermas 1988/1996, p.481) Spontaneous association is due not to an interest in the useful exchange of goods but the willingness to solve problems and coordinate action through mutual understanding.

Media-steered interactions in economic and administrative systems are defined by an uncoupling from members' values and goals. It seems an inversion of ends and means since administration takes on a life of its own. There is a self-programming circulation of power. Before taking on their own functions, power and law must fulfill functions for each other. "Law, which borrows its coercive character from power, first bestows on power the legal form that provides power with its binding character." (Habermas 1988/1996, p.482) Laws require a normative justification, while power is instrumental and policies function as a means for and a constraint on reproducing power. Power would not see the point of arguing a policy that is already determined. But we can only secure the rationality of decision making if parliamentary deliberations do not proceed by ideologically pre-given assumptions.

Deliberation and its "Dangers"

The public sphere generates the pool of reasons from which administrative decisions can draw their rationalizations. "Normative reasons can achieve an indirect steering effect only to the extent that the political system does not, for its part, steer the very production of these reasons." (Habermas 1988/1996, p.484)

> Civil Society can directly transform only itself, and it can have at most an indirect effect on the self-transformation of the political system; generally, it has an influence only on the personnel and programming of this system. (Habermas 1996, p.372)

Fobel did not talk about the relation between the "formally structured political will-formation and the surrounding environment of unstructured processes of opinion-formation." (Habermas 1988/1996, p.485)

> "Offensively" these movements attempt to bring up issues relevant to the entire society, to define ways of approaching problems, to propose possible solutions, to supply new information, to interpret values differently, to mobilize good reasons and criticize bad ones. ... "Defensively," they attempt to maintain existing structures of association and public influence, to generate subcultural counterpublics and counterinstitutions, to consolidate new collective identities, and to win new terrain in the form of expanded rights and reformed institutions. (Habermas 1996, p.370)

The public sphere is not programmed to reach decisions and therefore is not organized. The institutions and legal guarantees of free and open opinion-formation rest on the unsteady ground of the political communication of actors who, in making use of them, at the same time interpret, defend, and radicalize their normative content. Actors know they are involved in the common enterprise of reconstituting and maintaining structures of the public sphere as they contest and strive for influence. Their fallible outcomes however do have the presumption of practical reason on their side. New social movements are having a less-conspicuous but still dynamic impact on wide swaths of the public, giving rise to a hope for a healthy public sphere.

Autonomous public spheres must eventually take shape in democratic institutions because important decisions demand clear accountability. The informal opinion-making must be translated to the formal institutional will-formation of a majority vote. The public sphere influences the premises of judgment and decision making in the political system without trying to conquer it. From the pool of reasons that administrative power can handle instrumentally but cannot ignore, parliament must remain sensitive to autonomous public spheres. Opinion-forming associations develop in virtue of their visibility to change the values, issues, and reasons for wide sections of the populace. This will both innovatively unleash and critically filter the discourse channeled by the mass media. "Such a network of associations remains dependent on a liberal-egalitarian political culture sensitive to problems affecting society as a whole." (Habermas 1988/1996, p.488)

"The overextended project of a self-organizing society, so the argument goes, carelessly disregards the weight of traditions, organically developing reserves and resources that cannot be created at will." (Habermas 1988/1996, p.488) Constitutional democracy is now a project, both an outcome and accelerating catalyst of rationalization beyond politics into the lifeworld which meets it halfway. The sole aim is the gradual improvement of procedures for rational collective will-formation that do not prejudge the participant's concrete goals. The purpose is "realizing the system of rights anew in changing circumstances, that is, to interpret the system of rights better, to institutionalize it more appropriately, and to draw out its contents more radically." (Habermas 1996, p.384) To more fully utilize, expand, and radicalize existing communication rights and structures in the service of specific functions.

But "without the support of the sociopolitical culture, which cannot be produced upon command, the forms of communication adequate to practical reason cannot emerge." (Habermas 1988/1996, p.489) Elites may think this means the sovereignty of the people should be relocated to the opinion-forming avante-gardes. Problem is communicative power is only possible under conditions that exclude a concentration of power. We still require "a background political culture that is egalitarian, divested of all educational privileges, and thoroughly intellectual." (Habermas 1988/1996, p.490)

Civil Society and

the Political Public Sphere

The public sphere detects and identifies problems, amplifying their pressure by convincingly and influentially thematizing them, giving them workable solutions and dramatizing them in a way that they get taken up by parliamentary debates and made into legislation. Political influence ultimately rests on the resonance and approval of a lay public with an egalitarian composition, convinced by comprehensible and interesting contributions to issues they find relevant. Interest groups convert their social power into political power only so far as they can "advertise their interests in a language that can mobilize convincing reasons and shared value orientations." (Habermas 1996, p.364) The public sphere is made up of private persons coming together as a public. "For the public sphere draws its impulses from the private handling of social problems that resonate in life histories." (Habermas 1996, p.366) Socially generated problems can be assessed in terms of one's own life history. Civil Society is the social component of the lifeworld. It is spontaneously emergent associations attuned to how society's problems resonate in private life that distill, transmit, and amplify them to the public sphere.

This does not seem like our public sphere "dominated by mass media and large agencies, observed by market and opinion research, and inundated by the public relations work, propaganda, and advertising of political parties and groups." (Habermas 1996, p.367) "These official producers of information are all the more successful the more they can rely on trained personnel, on financial and technical resources, and in general on a professional infrastructure." (Habermas 1996, p.376-7)

> Because the public's receptiveness, cognitive capacity, and attention represent unusually scarce resources for which the programs of numerous "stations" compete, the presentation of news and commentaries for the most part follows market strategies. Reporting facts as human-interest

> stories, mixing information with entertainment,
> arranging material episodically, and breaking down
> complex relationships into smaller fragments – all
> of this comes together to form a syndrome that
> works to depoliticize public communications.
> (Habermas 1996, p.377)

As long as mass media draw their material from powerful well-organized information producers and prefer strategies that lower rather than raise the discursive level of public communication, issues will begin at and be managed by the center. Yet, "power relations shift as soon as the perception of relevant social problems evokes a crisis consciousness at the periphery." (Habermas 1996, p.382)

> The communication structures of the public sphere
> are linked with the private life spheres in a way
> that gives the civil-social periphery, in contrast to
> the political center, the advantage of greater
> sensitivity in detecting and identifying new
> problem situations. The great issues of the last
> decades give evidence for this. ... Hardly any of
> these topics were initially brought up by exponents

of the state apparatus, large organizations, or functional systems. Instead, they were broached by intellectuals, concerned citizens, radical professionals, self-proclaimed "advocates," and the like. Moving from this outermost periphery, such issues force their way into newspapers and interested associations, clubs, professional organizations, academies, and universities. They find forums, citizen initiatives, and other platforms before they catalyze the growth of social movements and new subcultures. The latter can in turn dramatize contributions, presenting them so effectively that the mass media take up the matter. Only through their controversial presentation in the media do such topics reach the larger public and subsequently gain a place on the "public agenda." Sometimes the support of sensational actions, mass protests, and incessant campaigning is required. (Habermas 1996, p.381) Civil disobedience summons public opinion against the systemic inertia of institutional politics.

Discursive Ethics

In strategic action a speaker seeks to influence the addressee by threats or bribes to continue their interaction the way the speaker wants. Such people care more about perlocutionary effects than the illocutionary speech act. It is very transactional, and consists of kickbacks and sanctions using power or money. This is the kind of reasoning studied by Public Choice. Communicative action on the other hand, seeks to rationally motivate the other by relying on the illocutionary binding/bonding effect of a speech act offer, a guarantee that if necessary the speaker will redeem the claim by giving reasons. It is a criticisable validity claim. As soon as the addressee accepts the offer, obligations are assumed that have consequences for the interaction which effect the coordination between those in dialogue and make its continuation possible.

Agreement means having the assent of all who might be affected. True impartiality generalizes those norms that can count on universal assent because they embody a common interest for all affected. It is these that deserve intersubjective recognition. This forces those affected to adopt the perspectives of everyone else affected in balancing all our interests. Agreement is possible when everyone's concerns are regulated in the equal interest of each person. We must seek real agreement.

All contents no matter how fundamental must be made to depend on real discourses. The moral theorist may take part but they cannot conduct such discourses by themselves alone. The revision of values that interpret our needs and wants cannot be handled by an individual inside their head but requires the cooperative effort and process of actual argument. I must submit my maxim to all others to discursively test its claims to universality, to what all can will as a universal norm. Habermas thought Rawls in *A Theory of Justice* (1971) was too monological, he came across as an expert with his own theory of justice to apply, but he later overcame his individualist slant when he moved on to the idea of public reason. Only an intersubjective process of reaching understanding can produce an agreement that is reflexive in nature and give the participants knowledge they have collectively become convinced of something.

Not just anything goes. There can be 'performative contradictions,' where what someone is saying undermines their position like the liar's paradox: 'everything I say is a lie.' If everything you said is a lie, then even that statement itself is a lie so it can't be true, but then since it *is* a lie the statement is true which it can't be. Seen another way, one cannot 'convince' someone else with lies. There is an internal connection in the meaning of 'to convince' with 'to come to a reasoned agreement about something,' such that convictions only rest on a consensus that has been attained through free and informed discussion. You can never *convince* someone by lies, you can only talk them into believing something not true. Similarly, one also cannot say "having excluded certain people from the discussion by silencing them or thrusting our interpretation upon them we were able to convince ourselves that we were justified." The content of the speech act contradicts the presuppositions of justification, which are not only true for that particular instance but for every process of argumentation. This gives us a transcendental-pragmatic justification for universal linguistic rules that have normative content. Habermas mentions three rules or presuppositions for the process of argumentation.

1. Deliberation is open to everyone without exception who can contribute.
2. Everyone must have equal opportunity to put forth their own arguments.
3. No speaker may be prevented by coercion from exercising these rights. They must be immune from repression and inequality. The only force must be the unforced force of the better argument. This neutralizes all motives other than the cooperative search for truth.

Not all actual discourses conform to these rules, in all cases we have to be content with approximations. We must only assume these conditions are realized adequately enough for argument's sake. Institutional measures may be needed to more approximate these presuppositions; topics and contributions have to be organized, and the opening, adjournment, and resumption of discussions must be arranged. We have to differentiate between the rules of discourse and those conventions needed to institutionalize discourse.

> Those actors who are the carriers of the public sphere put forward "texts" that always reveal the same subtext which refers to the critical function of the public sphere in general. Whatever the manifest content of their public utterances, the performative meaning of such public discourse at the same time actualizes the function of an undistorted public sphere. (Habermas 1996, p.369)

Communication in the public sphere is inherently reflexive and constantly reflects on itself because the presuppositions of an unorganisable practice can only be really secured by the practice itself. The political public sphere is just one among many public spheres, just as civil society is separate from both government and the economy. Society is decentered in intersubjective networks of communication, not a whole social subject focused in any one place like the state or the constitution. It is not in the head of any collective or individual actors.

> On account of its anarchic structure, the general public sphere is ... more vulnerable to the repressive and exclusionary effects of unequally distributed social power, structural violence, and systematically distorted communication than are the institutionalized public spheres of parliamentary bodies. (Habermas 1996, p.307-8)

John Rawls

Political Liberalism

While Habermas is concerned about a constitutional democracy with a vibrant and autonomous public sphere, Rawls is interested in free and equal moral persons setting fair conditions for cooperating in a just democratic political society that has the rule of law.

Habermas wants to protect the lifeworld of the public sphere from the encroachments of money and power, as systems they are more informally utilitarian and transactional. They can get in the way of truth. Rawls on the other hand wants us to leave our controversial metaphysics at the door and give reasons for our political principles we sincerely believe others can accept, so we can move towards an overlapping consensus on the appropriateness of our institutions and rights, even if that means correcting them to do so.

Rawls makes a distinction between rationality and reasonableness. The reasonable is public in a way the rational is not. Rationality applies to a single unified agent seeking their own ends and interests. What is rational is how these interests and ends are adopted and affirmed, how they are given priority, and how they cohere with and compliment each other. Reasoning about the best means to achieve those ends is also rational. So far this covers the economic rationality of Public Choice. People may vote according their social and economic preferences and interests as well as their dislikes and hates as a public choice theorist might speculate. They may vote according to what they think is the whole truth, with which many disagree, without considering the public reasons everyone can accept. But to do either of these would not recognize the duty of civility. What is lacking is a moral sensibility for fair cooperation on terms that others, as equals, might reasonably be expected to endorse.

Being reasonable is when, among equals, people propose principles and standards as fair terms of cooperation and abide by them willingly, even when against their interests in particular situations, given the assurance others will also. Reciprocity is the willingness to put forth your claims in terms others can accept, consistent with their freedom and equality. "Public justification is not simply valid reasoning, but arguments addressed to others." (Rawls 1993, p.465) Kant had said giving people reasons was a way of respecting their free and equal rational autonomy. Given the assumptions of accepting a constitutional democracy with the rule of law, we can find our judgements converge enough so political cooperation based on mutual respect can be maintained over generations, and no one is dominated and manipulated or under the pressure of an inferior political or social position. Even given that everyone is reasonable there may still be good grounds for disagreement. Rawls calls these the burdens of judgement.

Rawls asks how can we agree on politics if everyone has a different ultimate philosophical/religious doctrine over which we disagree? He desired a purely political liberalism rather than a metaphysical one like Kant. Comprehensive doctrines have an ultimate idea of human nature and purpose and the meaning of life. Liberalism can be supported by an overlapping consensus of people who hold different comprehensive but reasonable views. Each can support constitutional rights for distinct reasons according to their doctrine. Some comprehensive ideologies like autocracy or dictatorship however are not compatible with a constitutional democracy. These are unreasonable.

According to Rawls, to use public reason, we should check our comprehensive views at the door, or the whole truth as we see it, and give non-comprehensive reasons for the rules and candidates we support. Fundamental ideas are supposed to be purely political, metaphysical doctrines are to play no role. Comprehensive views can be introduced if backed up later by public reasons. Or if political values rooted in comprehensive doctrines strengthens public reason itself, Rawls would allow it because a wholehearted commitment to ideas can give reasonable political conceptions a vital social basis of enduring strength and vigor.

Showing their faith supports constitutional democracies, believers in comprehensive doctrines can reveal they are not a threat to be feared. But no one can give another the right to impose their doctrine. Problem is many people find this truncating, outlawing some of their most cherished views from becoming publicly debated. Rawls was inspired by the separation of church and state. Most major religions support this, but many fundamentalists do not. But Rawls' theory of public reason *does* encourage deliberators to seek common ground and offer acceptable arguments for the common good, shunning those that are too sectarian or narrow.

The Idea of Public Reason

An idea of public reason fits in with constitutional democracy, which has a plurality of reasonable comprehensive doctrines. Reason is public in three ways: it is the considered reason of the public, it looks after the common good, and it is expressed in public. There is only one public reason and many non-public reasons. In civil society there are non-public reasons for churches, universities, scientific societies, and professional groups. They are public with respect to their members but not to political society and citizens more generally. Non-public reasoning according to Rawls also includes all the media.

An ideal conception of citizenship presents how things might be if a just and well-ordered society, defined as a fair system of cooperation, encouraged people to be that way. It is what is possible and can be, yet may never be. Public reason seeks to answer 'fundamental questions' about matters of constitutional essentials and matters of basic justice such as the particular statutes and laws enacted according to the constitution. Most political questions do not concern these fundamentals.

Public reason applies to citizens when they engage in political advocacy in the public forum, as members of political parties, as candidates in political campaigns in public oratory, party platforms, and political statements along with those who support them like campaign managers. It not only governs the public discourse of elections if they involve the fundamental questions, but also how citizens cast their votes on these questions. It always applies to public and government officials in official forums, in their debates and votes on the floor of the legislature and executives in public acts and pronouncements. Public reason especially applies to the judiciary, above all the supreme court with judicial review. Justices have to explain and justify decisions based on the constitution and relevant statutes and precedents. Because the legislature and executive do not have to be justified in this way, the supreme court is the prime exemplar of public reason.

When may citizens properly vote to use their coercive political power on fundamental questions? In the light of what principles and ideals would make it justifiable to others as free and equal? As institutions and laws are imperfect so their discourse may be imperfect, how can it be reasonable or rational to appeal only to a public conception of justice and not to the whole truth as we see it? What about when the discourse is so shallow it does not set out the most basic grounds on which we believe our view rests?

> Since the exercise of political power must be legitimate, the ideal of citizenship imposes a moral, not a legal, duty – the duty of civility – to be able to explain to one another on those fundamental questions how the principles and policies they advocate and vote for can be supported by the political values of public reason. This duty also involves a willingness to listen to others and a fairmindedness in deciding when accommodations to their views should be reasonably made. (Rawls 1993, p.217)

We should be ready to accept reasonable alterations in our views; "opinions are not simply a fixed outcome of their existing private or nonpolitical interests." (Rawls 1997/2005, p.448) This preserves the ties of civic friendship. Legitimacy is inseparable from being justifiable to all citizens. We can only appeal to presently accepted general beliefs and forms of reasoning found in common sense, or the methods and conclusions of science if not controversial like disputed and elaborate theories of general equilibrium. "In securing the interests of persons they represent, the parties insist that the application of substantive principles be guided by judgement and inference, reasons and evidence that the persons they represent can reasonably be expected to endorse." (Rawls 1993, p.225) However everyone must be educated to acknowledge the concept of judgement, principles of inference, and rules of evidence, and must incorporate fundamental concepts of reason, including standards of correctness and criteria of justification.

There are many liberalisms and therefore many permissible forms of public reason specified by a family of reasonable political conceptions of justice. They all see citizens as free and equal persons and society as a fair system of cooperation over time. The government has a legitimate interest in seeing public law and policy support and regulate the institutions needed to reproduce political society and culture. New variants of conceptions of justice are proposed occasionally and old ones die out. This way the claims of groups or interests that arise from social change aren't repressed and fail to get their appropriate political voice. To engage in public reason is to appeal to one of the purely political conceptions of justice when debating fundamental political questions. We begin by working out the basic ideas of a complete political conception of justice that can answer our fundamental questions, and from there elaborate its principles and ideals, then use the arguments they provide to derive policy. The details of the injunction to present proper political reasons has to be worked out in practice and cannot be governed by clear rules given in advance. How they work out depends on the nature of public political culture, calling for good sense and understanding. The social role of a concept of justice is to enable all citizens to make mutually acceptable shared institutions and social arrangements by citing publicly recognized and sufficient reasons identified by that conception.

Whether the doctrine that results fulfills its purpose is decided by how it works out, whether after much consideration we can acknowledge it. A conception of justice fulfills its social role when citizens are equally conscientious and, sharing roughly the same beliefs, find that by affirming the framework of deliberation (a constitutional democracy with the rule of law) they are led to a convergence of opinion. It only has to be precise enough so we can justify to each other our common institutions. Principles must be easy to understand and simple to apply. Sharp and definite conclusions are not needed if sufficient agreement is forthcoming. At best a conception of justice can establish only a guiding framework for deliberation. A loose framework for deliberation must rely heavily on our powers of reflection and judgement. These are not fixed but are developed and shaped by a shared public culture.

What makes values uniquely those of public reason are they can only be realized in and characterize political institutions. Reasonableness and a readiness to honor the duty of civility, as virtues, make the public discussion of political questions possible. The immediate implications are the needs for the public financing of elections, and providing public occasions for the orderly and serious discussion of fundamental questions and issues of public policy. It needs to be set free from the curse of money. Corporate and other organized interests who contribute large donations to campaigns distort if not preclude public discussion and deliberation. In the constant pursuit of money to finance campaigns the political system is unable to function. Therefore, public inquiry must be free and public, and everyone must be given a decent education. Citizens support public reason when they hold politicians accountable to it.

Sharpening the Contrast between

Economics and Politics

Public reason is important for deliberative democracy because we are to give each other arguments the other can accept. Elizabeth Anderson and Philip Pettit contrast deliberative democracy to economic rationality. Anderson argues democratic ideals must be determined in public forums to which all have access. This entails having a voice in publicly arguing for one's position, and no one is excluded. Philip Pettit argues we need open avenues for contesting government decisions so the law does not arbitrarily dominate us but tracks our interests and values. We can change our priorities as the result of free and equal deliberation, while in economic bargaining ends are exogenously given and enforcing the contract depends on people's relative bargaining power.

Elizabeth Anderson

Elizabeth Anderson (1993) distinguishes between market goods and public goods such as fraternity and freedom. 'Fraternity' is when people agree to not make claims to certain goods at the expense of those less fortunate, and that this contributes to their own good. Fraternity is expressed by providing common goods by the whole community to its members. It erases any connection between specific donors and specific recipients. 'Freedom' is the ability to participate as equals in the cooperative project of self rule deciding laws and policies that govern us all. This means we should have what we need to effectively participate, such as education. These needs are to be met through community guarantee or direct provision, and are subject to democratic deliberation. People in a fraternal relation cannot interact without a shared understanding of the common ideals. Democracy differs from the market in three ways, according to standards internal to the positive functions or virtues of each.

1. Citizens exercise their freedom through having a voice, not just being able to exit. It's the power to shape the background conditions of their interactions and the content of the goods they provide in common.

2. A democracy is supposed to distribute goods according to public principles rather than unexamined wants. Decisions must be justified in publicly acceptable terms.

3. Public goods are nonexclusive and provided to everyone, not just those who can pay.

In a market a seller respects a customer by not prying into their privacy. To respect a fellow citizen, one must take the reasons for their position seriously. To consult and respond to their judgements in a public forum and adopt it if it is the better argument. "Shared values can be realized only through nonexclusive distribution responsive to shared understandings of principles and needs arrived at through voice." (Anderson 1993, p.166) All this summarizes into the formula that democratic ideals must be determined in public forums to which all have access.

The analogy itself between economics and political deliberation misses the contrasting values between the two rationalities. Anderson explores two kinds of proposals that fail to recognize the difference between market and democratic goods. Market ideologists try to replace public goods with private ones or cash equivalents.

1. Privatization. Some forms of freedom can only be secured through having an institutional voice of goods for which public access is guaranteed. No one has to ask anyone's permission to drive on a public road. Taxation is a necessary cost to preserve this. Individual freedom is not always increased when the common is divided. Each person may be despot in their own territory but subject to someone else everywhere else. In a

public park where people are there anyway for several reasons there is room for rallies, and petitioners can gain signatures which would be intrusive at home. Political action in a park is a by-product that can rapidly and effectively generate support and concern among strangers on matters of public interest. If this park was replaced with a mall, the mall owners may not allow speech they find offensive or against their interests. The space is then depoliticized.

2. Cash equivalents. The voucher system provides parents with a fixed sum of money to be spent on the school of their choice. Schools would have to compete in offering options to parents. This could satisfy more wants.

   This replaces having a voice with the freedom to exit. Instead of discussing with other parents the proper goals and practices of education to arrive at common principles, the parent is free to take their child elsewhere. This seems to assume the education system is to cater to the given unexamined wants of parents for which no reasons can be offered. But our educational system is justified by reasoned ideals, such as the need to prepare children for responsible citizenship in fraternity with those of different classes, races, or ethnicities. There is a benefit to determining the shape of education through political institutions that offer a public forum. The market does not distinguish between reasoned ideals and unexamined wants, and reduces everything to isolated publicly unarticulated decisions. Democratic ideals should be determined in forums to which all have access. It is in everyone's interest what the next generation will become.

Vouchers promote the freedom of parents to indoctrinate their child rather than educate the child to think for themselves. The right of the parent does not include keeping children in perpetual subjection. The child should have some autonomy to grow.

Market ideologies define someone as free if they can express their preferences in using or exchanging private property without having to respond to the preference's of others. Individuals are free to value something as much as they want without judgement. This reduces values to bare preferences or taste.

When autonomy is reduced to the expression of preferences as identified by actual market choices, it doesn't get asked if these revealed preferences reflect the agent's considered attitude, irrational preferences, or the preferences of others. Theorists may not question the power struggles that pre-determine the individual's choice before they enter the market.

But in democratically curtailing the market, people exercise collective autonomy over the background conditions of their interactions as a fraternity of citizens, rather than competing isolated labourers unable to protect themselves. This may limit choices at any particular time but it expands them for a broader range of significant ones over time.

Philip Pettit

The differences in values and ways of negotiation/deliberation between the market and a democracy are expounded in Philip Pettit's *Republicanism* (1997). Neoliberals think the way to organize public life is to have a framework so things will happen according to reason, defined as preference satisfaction, even if and especially if each looks out only for themselves. The way to get the best public results is not to have citizens internalize the common good and deliberate how to promote it, but have everyone look after themselves and rely on the economic/legal framework to ensure everything leads to the maximum good. Positivism in political science defined representative democracy as a pluralism of conflicting interests. 'Bargaining' is the negotiation of compromises. Economic bargaining begins with pre-given desires defined as objective self-interests and trades concessions to reach a mutually beneficial agreement, with each looking to offer the least from themselves, and will contest a decision if it does not stick to the original contract and demands a concession the other is unwilling to make. Bargaining, therefore, is only feasible if one has enough negotiating power to threaten the other's compliance. Making self-seeking the motor of political life can subject the weak to the naked preferences of the strong who have more resources.

In deliberation, according to Pettit, we interrogate each other about the nature and importance of our concerns, converging on an answer as to what arrangement best answers the considerations everyone recognizes as relevant. (It is better to work by consensus, where we may not end up with our first choice but everyone can agree to it, rather than to vote and create exclusion with well-entrenched political oppositions.) There should be enough common ground for conversation, but short of complete agreement there must be room for challenging arguments that can be recognized as relevant by all sides. We can protest unsuitable reasons that do not answer very well all relevant considerations. Debate is open to anyone who can plausibly challenge a reasoned decision, it does not theoretically depend on having clout. Also, preferences are formed by deliberation, not given by self-interest. The common image of getting a proper hearing for some challenge to change our priorities involves a popular movement creating widespread controversy and debate followed by progressive legislative adjustment. It should be possible for people to coalesce around group identities that were once suppressed, or espouse various causes that were not salient, so they have the opportunity to bring others to their point of view. All this involves changing and evolving what we consider our interests.

Enabling a proper hearing that can change our priorities has implications for our institutions. Pettit wanted to ensure counter-majoritarian conditions where the more basic and important laws were not subject to straightforward majoritarian amendment. He argued it was Rousseau who had put the populist element into self-government, which was later revived by Hannah Arendt's ideal of participatory democracy. Pettit said the history of the origin of legislation in consensus was not what's important, but the modal counter-factual of being able to pass possible contestation. A law does not have to dominate if it stops some people from arbitrarily interfering with the choices of others. The government will not arbitrarily dominate if it tracks the opinions and interests of the population when it makes legislation. Even if the whole decision-making process does not involve any domination we may still come up with a law that does. Pettit wants avenues to be open for contesting the decisions of government, such as writing a letter to one's member of Parliament, getting an inquiry by an ombudsman, or appealing to a higher court. Or, activities involving our rights of association, protest, and demonstration.

A tradition can always go through an epistemic crisis in which it may be retained, modified, or discarded. This is forever a possibility as long as the tradition is alive. We could always be wrong and not know it until it was brought to our attention somehow. This is forever an open issue, a necessary possibility. That is why the ability to contest public decisions is so important. We should always be willing to test ourselves and improve. Perfection is infinite, we can always learn. Intellectual integrity has the need to actually be right, regardless of what one wants to be true.

Internal Goods

Tullock argued that when forced to choose we should further the rational self-interest of our career over doing what's good for the organization or our boss. I would say that what we do is more important than what we get. Maximizing our benefits orient us to consequences rather than who we are or want to be. This takes us right to the heart of integrity and authenticity, being true to yourself. Doing something well something well worth doing. We must be true to the practice, such as telling the truth, and that means being true to the standards and values internal to our practices. It is a vital part of being a citizen to fight ignorance and take the effort to be informed. This is valuable for its own sake, whatever else we might get from it.

'Practices' are "a coherent and complex form of socially established cooperative human activity" (MacIntyre 1981, p.187). Most importantly in practices "goods internal to that form of activity are realized in the course of trying to achieve those standards of excellence which are appropriate to and partially definitive of that form of activity." (MacIntyre 1981, p.187) The values internal to our practices as forms of life motivate us to excel at the practice, systematically advance it, and keep it integral. Striving for the best of that practice "human powers to achieve excellence, and human conceptions of the ends and goods involved, are systematically extended." (MacIntyre 1981, p.187) It is open-ended, our understanding of normative principles can be infinitely fine tuned, we can always learn more thereby redefining our priorities.

The virtues of justice, honesty, and courage[5] help fight the temptations inherent in our institutions (power, wealth, and fame) that are goods that can distract us from pursuing the standards internal to our practices. The 'hedonic treadmill' means that when one's condition

---

[5] The virtues of justice, honesty, and courage support each other. Justice is to give to each their due, credit or blame. But to be just, we must first be honest with others and ourselves. Where do the boundaries of blame lie? Abuse thrives in secrecy and denial. To be honest takes courage, since it can threaten our self-image, and sometimes our virtues call upon us to risk our personal wealth, power, and fame.

permanently improves; one is excited for a while but then one's mood reverts back to a normal 'set-point.' This seems to be true more for external goods like wealth, power, or fame where how well off we are is determined by how we compare to others, since rising expectations can decrease overall satisfaction. In contrast, values pursued for internal reasons such as having close social relationships, improving oneself as a person, or contributing to the community are more sustainable sources of happiness, and the benefit to one is a benefit to all (Ahuvia and Izberk-Bilgin 2013).

We are called upon to put the goods of the community and our practice before the external goods of power, wealth, or fame. This is how we define integrity, putting the work and the standards internal to it as a practice over any distracting temptations to put yourself or your company first before serving the work itself and doing the best job one can.

Dorothy Sayers (1942/2002) has warnings for communitarians who would veer from putting the integrity of the work first. To aim at pleasing the community first is to falsify the work. It is the work that serves the community, and it is the worker who serves the work. One cannot do decent work if you take your mind off it to see how the community is taking it. If one's heart is not totally in the work it will not be good and will therefore serve neither God nor the community. The work has been falsified to please the public, and in the end the public is not pleased. Before pleasing our bosses and furthering our careers, we need to put the integrity of the work first. If we put the work before ourselves and our profit, we will not be anxious to please nor afraid to displease anyone. This takes balance since one must still try to please the client or customer; we have to anticipate their needs and rush to their aid. But this should still be done according to standards internal to the work itself and not compromised.

In 'Why Work?' (1942/2002) Sayers applies the Christian attitude to work as a calling and not just something for which we get paid. It is something we should do for its own sake. The worker's first duty is to serve the work itself. Nothing can make up for work that is not true to itself, work that is untrue to its own technique and living a lie. Goods are not to be valued for what they can fetch but if they do the job. We should fight for the quality of work we do. It should be worth doing, something in which we can take pride. The only reward work can really give is the satisfaction of its perfection. We should give work the same loving attitude we give our hobbies. It is only when work is looked upon as a means to gain that it becomes hateful. What we do is more important than what we get. Maximizing our benefits orients us to consequences rather than who we are or want to be. The heart of integrity and authenticity is being true to yourself. Doing something well something well worth doing.

This is the opposite of the lack of integrity in furthering our careers before doing what's best for our boss or organization. This strict definition of rationality as being career motivated is questionable because it does not put the work first and stay true to the standards internal to that practice. It is false to itself. But this is never questioned. Now Tullock (1965) does admit that one has to balance flattery with good performance. Someone who is charming and inefficient is as little likely to get promoted as an efficient boor. Therefore, an intelligent ambitious politician should do a respectable job regardless. MacIntyre would say that furthering one's career first is to fall into the temptation of wealth and power, a distraction from integrally pursuing the standards internal to our work which benefit everyone not just the person trying to keep up with the Joneses. It takes our eyes off the real prize.

William Riker's model favours those who want to win for its own sake, but there is a tendency to over-spend on victory. This uses up the leader's resources until they are bankrupt and this, in turn, will change the weight of everything in the system causing great disequilibrium. The politician should look beyond their own benefit, whether it's power, prestige, or continuing in their position. If the politician paid more attention to the actual worth of their policy and the service it provides for the people, instead of concentrating on always winning more, they would not overspend themselves to their ruin. Such a politician lacks integrity again because they are putting their own personal winning before serving the public.

There is a conflict of interests when one kind of good such as truth or service is corrupted by another such as personal gain. Ignorance, when it is people being paid to put out falsehoods disguised as truths, is a matter of putting profits before intellectual honesty. Or, the conflicts of interests whenever intellectuals act as mercenary apologists for whoever hires them, which is the result of subjugating research to the market. Or, when it is a matter of cutting information costs and is putting laziness over patriotism. All these are moral failings and lack integrity which we define as remaining true to the standards internal to our work. Subordinating the truth to the market lacks integrity, because it is not being true to the standards internal to the search for truth which is supposed to be the purposes of our news services and universities. Economizing on the effort of doing personal research can similarly lack integrity if the issue is important enough. Having a lack of integrity *is being* morally compromised, which can be missed by a value-neutral science. We end up with Tullock's Machiavellianism, ruthless calculating opportunism.

Constructivist Metaethics

Habermas

To those who say there is no morality, that everything is power. Habermas would say, "If you really believe that, then what you just said must not be a truth claim that you really believe in and

> are trying to convince me of with good reasons. Instead, it must be your act of power to get me to say something, regardless of whether it's true or not." [This is strategic action.] ... If there is no morality, I can't expect you to be sincere or to agree out of belief in the truth of the reasons you give. [This is a performative contradiction.] (Cahoone 2014, p.261-2)

However, Habermas was not a moral realist or ethical naturalist, which he saw as inherently conservative, holding some things to be beyond question or alteration. Constructivism is characteristic of Enlightenment inspired rationalism, which tries to determine the correct method by which we can reliably and fairly construct a proper result that didn't exist before. It relies on a decision procedure to determine if something is correct and assumes a neutral amoral universe otherwise. Habermas' inspiration came from the French Revolution.

The French Revolution was about more than just institutionalizing equal liberties. It was conscious of *being* a revolution, while the American Revolution was merely the outcome of events. The revolutionary consciousness created a new mentality with three elements: a historical discontinuity that broke with the traditionalism of nature-like continuities, the political practice of self-determination and self-actualization, and a trust in rational discourse to rationally critique and legitimate political authority. "Under these three aspects, a radically this-worldly, postmetaphysical concept of the political penetrated the consciousness of a mobilized population." (Habermas 1988/1996, p.467) Political force can no longer can be justified religiously by appealing to divine authority nor metaphysically as an ontologically grounded natural law. Politics has to be justified solely based on reason with the tools of postmetaphysical theory.

For Habermas norms are not facts. The social reality we address in regulative speech acts have an intrinsic link to normative validity claims and are not constituted independently. Norms must have actors to follow and fulfill them, while facts exist independently from being formulated by true propositions. Norms that are accepted do not necessarily mean they are valid, while a norm with a redeemable validity claim may not meet with any actual approval or disapproval. And, just because a law is in place does not mean it will continue to be accepted. A norm depends on being acknowledged by those it addresses, and if recognition depends on the expectation that a validity claim can be redeemed with reasons, then there is a connection between the "existence" of norms and the anticipated justification of corresponding 'ought' statements. While there is no such inner connection between facts and the expectations by a certain group that such statements can be justified.

When skeptically charged with relativism a moral cognitivist can respond with a transcendental justification. Regardless of context every argumentation rests on pragmatic presuppositions. These principles are not open to proof however. They are presuppositions, not conclusions. They must be logically assumed if we are to engage in a mode of thought essential to rational life. They are not exactly true but neither are they mere social convention nor free personal decisions. Universalization is implied by the presuppositions of argumentation in general, which is supposed to produce intrinsically cogent arguments with which we can redeem or repudiate claims to validity. The procedural norms Habermas argues for may not be compatible with all substantive legal and moral principles, but they do not prejudge substantive regulations. Habermas thinks there is no need for discourse ethics to have the status of an ultimate justification. "Constitutional rights and principles merely explicate the performative character of the self-constitution of a society of free and equal citizens." (Habermas 1996, p.384)

Habermas makes three points about the difference between *moralitat* or universal morality and *sittlichkeit* or substantive ethical life.

1. Discourse ethics is purely formal. It provides no substantive guidelines only the procedure of practical discourse, which is not for generating justified norms but for testing the validity of norms that are being proposed and hypothetically considered. Content has to be brought from outside. "It would be utterly pointless to engage in a practical discourse without a horizon provided by the lifeworld of a specific group and without real conflicts in a concrete situation in which the actors consider it incumbent upon them to reach a consensual means of regulating some controversial social matter. … [A]ntecedent disruptions determine the topics that are up for discussion." (Habermas 1983, p.103)

2. The universalization principle sharply separates evaluative statements from strictly normative ones, between the good and the just. Cultural values are so intertwined with the totality of a particular form of life that they cannot claim normative validity in the strict

sense.[6] By their very nature, cultural values are at best candidates for embodiment in norms that are designed to express a general interest. Deontology covers only those practical questions that can be debated rationally with the prospect of consensus; the normative validity of norms and not value preferences.

3. Ideas of the good life shape the identities of groups and individuals in a way that forms an integral part of their culture or personality. Moral questions on the other hand can in principle be decided rationally in terms of justice or the generalizability of interests. The good life is accessible to rational discussion only within the unproblematic horizon of a concrete historical form of life or conduct of an individual life. Rationality is increased when we isolate issues of justice. But practical judgements derive both their concreteness

---

[6] In Exemplarist Moral Theory (2017) Linda Zagzebski shows that instead of merely valuing a person's character trait we can value the person themselves, in the way they inspire us to demand more of ourselves. We are more sure that certain people *are* admirable than we are about what makes them so.

and power to motivate from unquestioning ideas of the good life and its *sittlichkeit*. Kohlberg's highest stage of moral development is post-conventional where moral judgement is dissociated from local conventions and any historical colouration of a form of life. Such people lose the naïve self-certainty of their lifeworld background as well as the thrust and efficacy of empirical motives.

Norms as rational imperatives are supposed to transcend this, but universal moralities depend on rationalized forms of life that make possible the prudent application of insights and the motives for translating those insights into action. According to Habermas only those forms of life that meet the universal halfway can reverse the abstractive achievements of decontextualization and demotivation.

Rawls' Political Constructivism

Public principles of justice founded on the principles and conceptions of practical reason is of great significance for a constitutional regime. Rawls' theory tries to bring to awareness a conception of the person and social cooperation implicit in a democratic culture, or at least congenial to its deepest tendencies when properly expressed and presented. In this way he doesn't just make it up. But principles are not independent of our conceptions of a person and justice, nor are the same principles true in all possible worlds. Principles of justice are not so much true as reasonable, given our conception of persons as free and equal cooperating members of a democratic society. How are fair terms for cooperation to be determined? Laid down by some outside authority, or in view of knowledge of an independent moral order? Given the fact of reasonable pluralism citizens cannot agree on any moral authority, nor do they agree about the order of moral values. A shared political life appeals to the value of political life conducted on terms that all reasonable citizens can accept as fair. This leads to democratic citizens settling their fundamental differences in accordance with an idea of public reason. Rawls contrasted himself to rational intuitionism for its metaphysical realism, and Kantian constructivism because it is a comprehensive doctrine, then went on to define as 'objective' reasons sufficient to convince all reasonable people.

Rational Intuitionism

Rawls' political constructivism differs from the realism of rational intuitionism in many ways.

1. Intuitionism says moral first principles and judgements, when correct, are true statements about an independent order of moral values that do not depend on the activity of our reason. While political constructivism thinks the principles of political justice are the outcome of a procedure of construction. "It claims only that its procedure represents an order of political values proceeding

from the values expressed by the principles of practical reason, in union with conceptions of society and person, to the values expressed by certain principles of political justice." (Rawls 1993, p.95)

2. Intuitionists hold moral knowledge is gained by a kind of perception as well as first principles found on due reflection. Rawls bases construction on practical not theoretical reason. The former is concerned with the production of products like a constitutional regime, the latter is concerned with knowing these objects.

3. Intuitionists require only a conception of the person as a knower. They assume that an intuitive knowledge of first principles will give rise to a desire to act for their sake. Constructivism uses a more complex conception of the person and society to give form and structure to its construction. That is debateable, but it could be relative to what was then hegemonic, the intuitionism of G. E. Moore (1903) that defined metaethics.

4. Intuitionists see moral judgements as true when they are both about and accurately correspond to the independent order of moral values, or else they

are false. Rawls contrasts this to being reasonable, being willing to propose fair terms of cooperation among equals, and a willingness to accept the consequences of the burdens of judgement. The idea of the reasonable makes an overlapping consensus of reasonable doctrines possible in ways the concept of truth may not.

5. Both intuitionism and constructivism rely on reflective equilibrium. The intuitionist regards a procedure as correct because following it reliably gives a correct judgement about an independent reality. Political constructivists see a judgement as correct when it issues from the reasonable and rational procedure of construction when correctly formulated and followed. For intuitionists an error is a mistake in correspondence, for constructivists the fault lies in the constructive procedure itself.

Rawls used to believe there was no place in constructivism for approximating moral truth since there are no such moral facts to approximate.

[P]arties are not required to apply, nor are they bound by, any antecedently given principles of right and justice. Or, put another way, there exists

no standpoint external to the parties' own
perspective from which they are constrained by
prior and independent principles in questions of
justice that arise among them as members of one
society. (p.251)

As free and rational persons, members of a well-ordered society "think of themselves not as inevitably tied to the pursuit of the particular final ends they have at any given time, but rather as capable of revising and changing these ends on reasonable and rational grounds." (Rawls 1980/1997, p.250)

The principles of right and the good were not for him epistemological issues since they were not cases of knowledge at all. Later he was at pains to show political constructivism does not contradict intuitionism. "We do not say that the procedure of construction makes, or produces, the order of moral values." (Rawls 1993, p.95) The intuitionist says this order is independent and constitutes itself. Rawls neither affirms nor denies this. He merely does not want to speculate about knowing true moral facts. He does not want to get metaphysical. The concept of the reasonable suffices and is most appropriate for a pluralist democratic society. It provides the most reasonable conception of justice as the focus of an overlapping consensus. Reaching reasonable agreement replaces the search for moral truth.

Kantian Moral Constructivism

Rawls came up with the term constructivism with his three lectures 'Kantian Constructivism in Moral Theory' (1980). He later became eager to distance himself from Kant's metaphysical theory. Kant had a doctrine that was a comprehensive moral view with a regulative role for autonomy for all of life. For Rawls, a comprehensive liberalism based on autonomy can belong to a reasonable overlapping consensus that endorses a political conception, but it would still not be suitable to provide a public basis for justification. A political view has 'doctrinal autonomy' if it represents or displays the order of political values as based on principles of practical reason in union with the appropriate political conceptions of person and society. A deeper meaning of 'constitutive autonomy' has the order of moral or political values being constructed by the principles and conceptions of practical reason. Rawls holds it was Kant's idea that the so called independent order of values does not constitute itself but is constituted by practical reason itself. Principles of practical reason originate in our moral consciousness as informed by practical reason. It is self-originating and self-authenticating. Kantian constructivism sees itself as the defense of a constitutional democratic regime. Rawls did not think we needed to get as metaphysical as Kant's comprehensive doctrine of Idealism. This marks a radical shift from his earlier skeptical stand to a stronger more ontologically neutral position.

Conceptions of Person and Society

'Society' is one whose members engage in activities guided by officially recognized rules that those cooperating accept and regard as properly regulating their conduct. It is to be a fair system of cooperation from one generation to the next within a certain well-defined territory. 'Persons' are free and equal, rational and reasonable, with a sense of justice and a conception of the good, as well as determinate final ends and attachments. The principles of practical reason as both reasonable and rational compliment our conceptions of person and society. The conceptions of society and person are not constructed so much, but are rather assembled and connected.

Rawls' understanding of the original position, however, is still too theoretically thin since his model represents persons as solely free and equal moral persons with nothing substantive characterizing them. Behind a 'veil of ignorance' persons are not to know their place in society, nor their place in the natural lottery of talents and abilities. They do not know what their conception of the good is, their particular final ends, or their distinctive psychological dispositions and propensities. Rawls simply held his conception was implicitly affirmed by democratic culture.

Justice as Fairness

Justice as fairness aims at uncovering a public basis of justification on questions of political justice given the fact of reasonable pluralism. What is constructed is the content of a political conception of justice as selected by parties in the original position. Is the original position itself constructed? No. We start the fundamental idea of society as a fair system of cooperation between reasonable and rational free and equal persons. Then lay out a procedure that exhibits reasonable conditions to impose, such as the symmetry of equality and limits on self-information. This is required so no one is advantaged, or not, in their disparate bargaining positions of adopting principles, by natural accident or social luck. Because of the original position persons are represented as situated equally and therefore fairly. The aim is to express in the procedure all relevant criteria of the reasonable and rational that apply to political justice. If done properly the argument from the original position should yield the most appropriate principles of justice to govern political relations between citizens. This way the political conception of citizens as cooperating in a well-ordered society shapes the content of political right and justice. "Not everything, then, is constructed; we must have some material, as it were, from which to begin." (Rawls 1993, 104) Only the substantive principles of political right and justice are constructed.

Objectivity

Rational intuitionism, Kantian constructivism, and political constructivism each have a conception of objectivity but understand this in separate ways. Intuitionism and political constructivism can agree there is no way of having well-grounded knowledge without reasoned discussion, though intuitionism appeals to moral perception in ways constructivism does not. Intuitionism may grant political constructivism has a kind of objectivity appropriate for its political and practical purposes. It is only that it does not see principles as true or false of an independent order of values. Constructivism neither asserts nor denies this idea of truth, because it goes beyond the bounds of a political conception of justice framed so far as possible to be acceptable to all reasonable comprehensive doctrines.

The political values of a constitutional democracy can be worked out using society as a fair system of cooperation between free and equal citizens as reasonable and rational. For a workable political conception, no more is needed than a public basis in the principles of practical reason with concepts of society and person. Reasonableness is the standard of correctness. Objectivity is the features required of a framework of thought and judgement if it is to be an open and public basis of justification for free and equal citizens. When citizens share a reasonable political conception of justice, they share a common ground on which to discuss fundamental questions. The essentials of objectivity are necessary for a shared public basis of justification and suffices for the purposes of a political conception of justice. It need not go beyond its reasonable judgement and can leave the concept of true moral judgement to comprehensive doctrines.

Political convictions are objective if reasonable and rational persons conscientious in exercising their practical reason eventually endorse them or significantly narrow their differences about them under conditions favourable to due reflection. To say this is objective is to say there are reasons sufficient to convince all reasonable people. "Given a background of successful practice over time, this considered agreement in judgment, or narrowing of differences, normally suffices for objectivity." (Rawls 1993, p.120) Much important disagreement is consistent with objectivity as per the burdens of judgement; such as difficulties in surveying and assessing all the evidence, or the delicate balance of competing reasons. "Disagreement may also arise from a lack of reasonableness, or rationality, or conscientiousness of one or more of the persons involved." (Rawls 1993, p.121) But we need an independent reason to believe this, other than the disagreement itself.

The facts relevant in practical reasoning are no more constructed than person and society. Constructivist procedure yields principles to identify which facts are relevant and to determine their weight. Facts about the political conception are not constructed but are about the possibilities of construction. Only the substantive principles of political right and justice are constructed.

Habermas acknowledged that the procedure of deliberation needs content from outside. The question is whether the pragmatic logic of discursive ethics has independent validity. One should judge a procedure by its results. But to declare there are moral facts to which we must approximate would be to predetermine one's line of inquiry when we should be willing to question ourselves and our assumptions. We are all supposed to be equal deliberators so there should be no real and valid reason why one person's opinion should overpower another's except the stronger argument, and nothing should restrict us from freely making up or changing our mind but the better argument. Nothing can limit the perfection for which we can reach. These are the great sins, or values that need to be protected, that lead constructivists like Rawls and Habermas to deny there are any moral facts. Rawls came to qualify this by taking an agnostic position on moral realism, because a negative stand could be controversial for different comprehensive doctrines, and he defined 'objectivity' as reasons sufficient to convince all reasonable people.

I think in some way he came to realize you can't prove a negative; you can't prove something doesn't exist because if it doesn't exist there is no proof. And the only way to prove someone is wrong when they say there are no moral facts is to show them some. Rawls' new agnosticism might allow for this as a theoretical possibility, but he would not want to get metaphysical. Since a double negative does not necessarily equal a positive, it is not enough to criticize the basis for their skepticism. You have to show them wrong by getting it right. So Part Three examines epistemology from the point of view of virtue realism, which has some implications for deliberative democracy in analyzing and dealing with today's culture of misinformation.

Part 3: Virtue Realism

You can keep the ideal of deliberative democracy without having to accept all the accompanying theoretical baggage such as constructivist metaethics. Instead 'critical thinking' and 'emotional intelligence' can take on substantive content as virtues that can characterize institutions and individuals when expressed as understanding and respect. Examining things from all sides and being willing to change one's mind as a result, while having the sensitivity to notice local differences in moods and intentions, can deeply affect others and are complimentarily suited to a democracy that deliberates. It takes into consideration the content of our inspirational feelings, which public choice and constructivism do not.

The problem is our emotional reactions are faster than our thoughts. We tend toward motivated reasoning where one has a confirmation bias for information that aligns with previous beliefs and a disconfirmation bias that dismisses contrary information. We live with echo-chambers of information silos that narrowcast to a limited audience, designed with social-media algorithms that present information similar to what has previously caught one's attention. Selective exposure and polarization in the environment can lead to extremism, to the point where we have dueling fact perceptions. One consequence of this is there is no accountability, partisan politicians can just deny the crime ever took place. In our consumption of information, we have to beware of our own prejudices. We need to ask ourselves whether our feelings are correctly based on reality or not? Perhaps the best way to test this is in discussing it with others.

A) The Basis of Virtue Realism

Historical Narrative and the Enlightenment Project

The most fundamental fact about humans is that life is full of ups and downs, highs and lows making up our personal histories. Alasdair MacIntyre (1981) argued we can only answer what we are to do when we understand what are the stories of which we are a part. We are already socialized into particular roles from which we begin. We start from where we are but we do not have to stay there. We can always change and improve. Through criticism and invention, the limitations of what has been is transcended. Life is a quest to discover what is the good life. We begin with a vague clue, but we can only fully articulate our goals after the journey. Traditions are defined by the answer they give to what are the goods that give a tradition its point and purpose. When alive traditions are full of conflicts and competing ideas that extend through generations, of which the individual's life is a part and gives the individual's life their significance.

Our goods and corresponding priorities have been redefined throughout history.

Actions are made intelligible within the context of the longer histories of numerous traditions.

> We cannot ... characterize behaviour independently of intentions, and we cannot characterize intentions independently of the settings which make those intentions intelligible both to agents themselves and to others. ... Without the setting and its changes through time the history of the individual agent and his changes through time will be unintelligible. (MacIntyre 1981, p. 206-7)

Having a sense of traditions would be a grasp of the future possibilities which the past makes available in the present.

MacIntyre sees history as involving narratives heading towards a *telos* or end point based on our traditions. Agents are not only actors playing their roles but co-authors of their dialogue, working in agreement or not. They have beginnings, middles, and endings. They embody reversals, recognitions, digressions and subplots.[7] In lived narratives, we don't know what will happen next and certain possibilities entice us while others repel us. The future is always viewed as a telos, a set of ends or goals towards which we are moving or not. We are moving toward a climax, a point, or not. This is a purely human element to be added to the indifferent procession of passing 'now' moments in the un-ending present, of just one meaningless thing meaninglessly following after another.

Charles Taylor (1989) wrote that we are called upon to narrate our life story. We cannot avoid asking if our life amounts to anything, or whether it is just one damn thing after another without any point. If we are not well situated in relation to the good, or we are digressing away from it, this can be devastating. The question as to

---

[7] "A narrative identifies episodes, phases, stages, steps, advances, setbacks, anticipations, turning points, watersheds." (Dray, 1993, p. 105).

200

which direction we are moving and how far we have to go is not an optional question we can avoid. It matters to us intensely. We understand who we are by understanding how we came to be where we are. Determining how genuine is our real growth depends on the struggles we have had to overcome. We can only argue for the greater value of some way of life by describing our life transitions toward greater understanding by articulating how one position identifies and resolves a contradiction or confusion the other relies upon, or acknowledges some good the other does not. However, if the origins of our attitudes can be reinterpreted as a deception or loss, we need to re-evaluate our plans and ideas. As we move forward in life we can continue to endorse our present direction and commitments, or choose to give our life new ones. What we cannot do without is the need for our life, as a whole, to have meaning, weight, and significance, and not just be a waste of time.

Virtue Realism

Historically, MacIntyre (1981) thought that culturally we once had a telos of ends and purposes of what we should be when we are fulfilling our potential. Virtues helped us get there. That was before the Enlightenment's attempt to reform society, without relying on traditions specific to a people's culture, such as constructivism. This resulted in a situation in which things have lost their function and no longer makes sense as if we were speaking babble. For both MacIntyre and Aristotle, the *arête* or excellence of any function is to perform that function well. This is its virtue. The function of a watch is to keep time, so a good watch keeps accurate time. This applies to all trades, as well as all our other roles, public or private, such as being married, parents, or friends.[8] Each

____

[8]Professions usually have very clearly defined responsibilities. Personal relationships are not so often explicitly defined, but they too have standards internal to their roles. According to Aristotle there were three kinds of friendship. One were the casual acquaintances we meet everyday at the store or office. The second is the people whose company we enjoy for its pleasure. The third and best is when friends are ones based on appreciating the other's virtue. I would say that in such cases each can help the other become more virtuous; they can

trade fulfills a role and if it fills that role well it is excellent. Virtues are the standards of excellence appropriate to and partially definitive of a particular form of activity. A functional concept derives what normatively 'should be' from a description of 'what is,'; A Captain ought to do what a Captain ought to do. Hume said this was impossible. Aristotle's ethics sought to provide the missing link between man as he is and man as he should be when he is fulfilling his potential. Virtue helps us get from here to there. Now because of instrumental reason, which says we can only rationally argue about the best means to given ends and not about the ends themselves, we find ourselves locked in an emotional stalemate beyond which we find it difficult to argue.

---

ask the right questions to help the other figure out for themselves what they should do next, encouraging the other to recognize their triumphs when they happen, while personally appreciating any progress the other makes. Parents must similarly be both loving and give guidance. They must allow the child some freedom to grow but they must also teach them to be sensitive and responsible. Marriages similarly have vows that define the relationship.

Virtue Realism

MacIntyre epitomizes the English Analytic tradition in its confrontation with history and ethics. He has been criticized for bringing history into ethical philosophy, and for brining analytic philosophy into history. William K. Frankena, an analytic philosopher, criticized Alasdair MacIntyre for bringing in irrelevant historical narratives. The history of ideas follows the rise and fall of concepts, while philosophy is concerned with standards of rationality and truth. If one has the right conceptual equipment one can tell what a moral theory is without seeing it as a historical development. One can also assess its status as true or false and rational to believe without seeing it as such an outcome. MacIntyre's criticism of emotivism and the understanding that the Enlightenment project of justifying morality had to fail has more to do with analytic philosophy than historical narrative. Historical enquiry is irrelevant. The claim is the historicist must make use of analytic non-historical standards to evaluate rational superiority. MacIntyre does not see using analytical techniques as detracting from his historicism. On the flip side of the spectrum, Abraham Edel criticizes MacIntyre for focusing too much on explicit theorizing, articulated concepts, and the stories told by the people affected to pay attention to actual social and institutional life. MacIntyre is also criticized by Edel for distorting the complex history of morality in favour of promoting Aristotle. While Frankena criticizes MacIntyre for being an inadequate analytic philosopher with an additional irrelevant interest in history, Edel saw MacIntyre as an inadequate social historian who keeps needlessly dragging in analytic philosophy.

MacIntyre adopts Thomas Kuhn's theory of scientific revolutions, which is a historical style of justification, to the tradition of virtue ethics. If a tradition can adapt and overcome its previous limitations, then it proves its ability to survive. MacIntyre shows his philosophical side in his history thesis in that he is primarily concerned to prove the rational superiority of the virtue tradition. History is exactly the means to show the evolution of thought and the ability of a tradition to adapt. The superiority of a theory to its rivals reveals itself in its ability to transcend limitations by solving problems in areas where predecessors and rivals could make no progress by their own standards. Rational superiority has to be shown historically, to show how rivals and predecessors have been challenged and displaced. Abstract from that context and one is confronted with insoluble incommensurability problems. It is important to know how adherents came to adopt and defend their views. If we see something like Newtonian physics as satisfying rationality-as-such then we will lose sight of what made it rationally superior over the only available alternatives in the seventeenth and eighteenth centuries. The goal is not to find a theory that cannot possibly be refuted, but to obtain the best theory so far. If a position transcends the limitation of its predecessors and offers the best means to understand them to date, or can modify itself to incorporate the strengths of rivals while avoiding their weaknesses and at the same time present the best explanation of those strengths and weaknesses, then we can be reasonably confident that future challenges will be successfully met by enduring principles.

The final principles we hope to achieve from living out our life history are not articulate scientific theories, but the blessing of the insight of *phronesis*, the intuition that results in/from finding the right patterns in our data of experiences. This can undergo a revolutionary transformation or gestalt shift, an 'aha!' moment at any time. Which is a revolutionary sensitivity that is infinite, we can always learn more. For MacIntyre, Aristotle's *phronesis* meant knowing 'how to exercise judgement in particular cases.' It is an intellectual virtue without which none of the virtues of character can be exercised. This entails an accurate perception of ethical saliences. Aristotle defined virtue as the input of feeling the right passions along with the output of choosing the right actions "at the right times, with reference to the right objects, towards the right people, with the right motive, and in the right way." It is to be what is both intermediate and best for the individual in that role. (Aristotle, 2009, pp. II:6b, 20-23) It is excellence in practical intelligence.

Practical Intelligence and the Virtues (2009) is a Neo-Aristotelean treatise in which Daniel C. Russell wrote "phronesis is part of flourishing because it is the excellence of the practical intellect, and thus of a crucial aspect of the human person." (Russell 2009, p.17) One deliberates to decide on particular actions. "Aristotle says that the intellectual virtues are all capacities by which we reason correctly and arrive at truth (NE VI.2, 1139a21-31)" (Russell 2009, p.15) In practical reason truth is what we have the most reason to do. Aristotle further said "we deliberate, not about ends, but about what forwards those ends." (NE III.3, 1112b11-2, 33-4) On a narrow reading, whether motivation comes from emotions outside the intellect, or from reason habituating our desires over time, they both hold that ends are not grasped by deliberation but are always already determinate; we do not deliberate about ends but about means.

However, according to Russell, in a broader reading "ends are not always already determinate, and deliberation also involves *specification* of ends." (Russell 2009, p.7) The quest for a good life is in answering the question 'what is a good life?' *Phronesis* "is the excellence of practical reasoning whereby one specifies the contents of one's ends well." (Russell 2009, p.8) Sometimes to specify one end is to choose another one. "'Living well' is an indeterminate end, and one that we achieve only by adopting and pursuing other ends." (Russell 2009, p.11) Having some personal sense of a good life is important in balancing different ethical concerns. "No virtue can function in isolation from other virtues, since it is not clear that an act can hit the mean of any virtue if it also fails with respect to some other virtue." (Russell 2009, p.30) In balancing the specific concerns we face within the circumstances of our life, we need to ask what would constitute good examples defining true virtue?

Plural Metaethical Knowledges

Moral knowledge combines natural, non-natural, and anthropocentric insights; just as virtues combine what we think, feel, and do.

The good is natural insofar as the excellence of any function is to perform that function well. This is its virtue, and is defined by the nature of whatever we are investigating; since the function of a watch is to tell time a good watch tells accurate time. Similarly, a captain ought to do what a captain ought to do. Virtues are defined by the various roles contingently discovered in society, rather than stipulated and constructed by us. No matter how precisely you define your terms you can't define things in and out of existence. The *Character Strengths and Virtues* handbook (2004) by Martin E. P. Seligman and Christopher Peterson, is a DSM like *The Diagnostic and Statistical*

Manual of Mental Disorders used by health care professionals as the authoritative guide to the diagnosis of mental disorders. Only this book is used for 'positive psychology,' the study of peak experiences. The text is a psychological categorization of good qualities or virtues. A lot of research and care went into defining the various virtues, presenting the list at conferences over a period of five years and refining it after group discussions with the participants.

Vague terms actually allow us to more closely approximate an initial awareness of what we are trying to investigate, allowing room to move toward more perceptive definitions. Definitions are not short analytic formulas like you find in a dictionary, but describe what characteristic qualities constitute a good example. As long as we have an initial grasp on something tangible we can come to a sharper awareness. For Linda Zagzebski (2017) virtue realism is based on a direct reference to an exemplar who illustrates through their life a true example of a particular virtue or collection of virtues. It is a part of our theoretical development and improvement to define our terms more sharply in accordance with the increasing awareness we have of the phenomenon we are observing. Superficial qualities can help us pick out a reference, from which we can investigate further to discover an underlying deep structure. Superficially, water is an odorless colourless liquid that flows in streams and falls from the sky. We later learned that the deep structure we were really referring to by the word 'water' was H_2O. Zagzebski argues that with virtues we are more sure of who is admirable than what makes them that way. By listing the superficial properties that inspire us, we can point to someone or something and reference them directly, and through empirical research we can come to a more specific structural formula that underlies why that person has those virtue or virtues. Perhaps finding some advice for helping us better live the virtue(s) ourselves. Just as new social developments have expanded and improved the understanding of our needs and capabilities, philosophers are encouraged to treat theoretical definitions as contingent, tentative, and revisable upon further experience and repeated observation; rather than pre-set in stone and dictating what is to be even considered an example.

Not all the properties of a natural kind will be present in all of its examples. We have to see. One person may need the virtue 'courage' to stand up while another must use it to back down. If two situations do not merit the same response, however, there should be some significant natural property that is different between them. Moral facts are *constituted* by natural ones. "It is just such social, political, and legal arrangements that constitute South Africa's racial injustice. It is impossible that these natural facts remain as they are but that racial injustice should fail to exist." (Brink, 1989, p. 191) But while you can't have a higher-level change without a lower-level event or change, that does not mean the lower-level event can explain the higher level one. "Supervenience asserts that while any change in mental events or properties must presuppose a change in neural events or properties, the mental events or properties could still not be reduced to, or explained by, neural events alone." (Cahoone 2010b, p.132) The higher level science has its own standards of validity, while still having a conservative ontology. Logic is universally valid and can even use mousetraps to express its relations. Virtues have non-natural ideals that supervene upon purely natural functions, giving them a point and future direction. Virtues are supposed to serve a good life.

The good is natural since it is found contingently defined in the human nature of our social world, but it is also non-natural since the good can transcend and criticize whatever is supposed to be put in its place, capable of infinitely refining our priorities and sensitivities. Living through all the trials, tribulations, and changes of our life the persistent goal is still to ultimately answer for ourselves the question 'what is a good life?' The good life is an everlasting quest for finding out what constitutes a good life. "'Living well' is an indeterminate end, and one that we achieve only by adopting and pursuing other ends." (Russell 2009, p.11) *Phronesis* "is the excellence of practical reasoning whereby one specifies the contents of one's ends well." (Russell 2009, p.8) This practical wisdom is what ultimately makes any virtue a virtue and gives it its point, a future direction for developing further. In the end a detail of any situation can always disqualify what at best can only be a 'rule of thumb;' something generally true but neither universally nor necessarily so. We can never know beforehand everything that would make a difference to our decision, but starting from wherever you happen to be you can use consistency to correct yourself, and through having discussions with others we can become aware of unforeseen implications, contradictions, or ambiguities.

Correcting oneself is an infinite task. When G. E. Moore says that after defining the Good as X, we can still validly ask whether X is actually 'good?' this points not towards another world, but to the element of infinity in all normative concepts. The chance of learning we are mistaken is forever a necessarily open possibility. We can always be wrong and not know it until we find out. Our understanding of normative principles can always be more finely tuned; we can always learn more, thereby redefining our priorities. We can even have our own valid interpretation of a virtue that is unique to us. Perfection as the continuous attempt to always improve is a never-ending task. It is infinite in breadth and scope as well as unlimited in potential and possibilities; and hence non-natural.

So much for our intellectual definitions of virtue in light of the ideals of a good life. Feelings, on the other hand, are anthropocentric reactions to our world that offer further 'moral' insights. If one does not have the right feelings or attitude one will not be able to see what is in front of their eyes. For the first time our emotions introduce moral considerations of good versus evil into what so far have been the merely natural goods and bads of functions, even when supplied with non-natural idealizations. Economists do not generally deal with something as nebulous as feelings. They prefer mathematical logic and precision. They want value-neutral science.

But we can never make explicit all the considerations a researcher relies upon to make educated guesses that pay off; scientific 'intuition' is developed by learning explicit theory as well as by training in all sorts of experimental practices. Similarly, moral judgments are a species of trained reactions based on observations. Initially we're forced to take a leap of faith on a strategy, followed by an intense emotional reaction to its consequences. This adds to the experience of the learner. After enough of these experiences we develop intuitions that shortcut deliberation. The virtuous expert keeps asking for more details until they can "see" what needs to be done in the unique situation. People who are indifferent to morals suffer a cognitive deficit, like a perceptual disorder. Without sympathy we will not be aware of moral facts that fail to motivate us, and we will lack a cognitive capacity that is ordinarily important for the correct assessment of moral facts.

For example, people enjoy the camaraderie they feel with those they spend time, as with the civic virtue of 'citizenship.' It feels good to be part of a team, to serve those with whom we belong. But this can be further divided into the good and bad. Loyalty is good but what matters most is the integrity and purpose of the group to which one is loyal. In good civil society, people see those with whom they deeply disagree as deserving respect, while bad civil society promotes hatred and bigotry. Evil is an anthropocentric value that adds to the merely natural flaws of failed functions. Hate causes strife and conflict, while respect promotes peace.

In a peaceful democracy 'goods' and ideals must be defined and justified in public forums to which all have access. Reality is intersubjective and not up to one man. Therefore, we need 'respect' for different opinions, realizing no one has the complete truth. Following Aristotle we can see the opposite of maximizing our own priorities is to balance the community's various goods so they compliment each other. Hannah Arendt (1958, p.243) defined respect as a kind of friendship without intimacy or closeness, and is independent of any achievements we may admire. It can forgive for the sake of the one forgiven.

We should ask if it is possible to justify our feelings by the actual presence of a moral property or not? And, what marks the property as appropriate for such a reaction? It is one thing to explain that we should not manipulate the emotions of others because this is what respecting their rights requires. It is another thing to spell out what makes people worthy of our respect and the higher mode of life and feeling involved in recognizing this.

> If you want to discriminate more finely what it is about human beings that makes them worthy of respect, you have to call to mind what it is to feel the claim of human suffering, or what is repugnant about injustice, or the awe you feel at the fact of human life." (Taylor, 1989, p. 8)

Our sense of what confers dignity upon us explains our deepest gut reactions, as well as what it means to respect that dignity. Articulating our background frameworks is to explain the picture that makes sense of our moral responses, the ontology assumed by our most automatic emotional reflexes. These must be based on reality.

In attempting to make explicit the moral point of our actions through describing the qualitative distinctions that motivate them, we can come up with a more perceptive description that moves us to accept the new description as our own, possibly inspiring us to do more than we thought we could. Since understanding moral terms is inseparable from being moved by them, we can say the virtuous person has a better grasp of the meaning of ethical concepts and ideas than those indifferent or weak-willed. In fact, the exceptionally virtuous may have their own nuance on what constitutes a particular virtue that is uniquely personal to them.

Having the right feelings can help us do our work, making it easier and run smoother, as well as giving us the perceptive discernment to motivate us to do it better. By means of discussion we can develop our focus and discriminate more keenly, making room for the discovery of further properties that are more remote; we can come to recognize we feel admiration rather than love or indignation rather than hate. Having a term for something enables us to have epistemic access to it, and sometimes it is enough just to adequately name the feeling so we can take a stand and react appropriately.

How should we put into practice the respect needed for deliberation in a decent democracy? What should we *do*? In civil society groups of citizens can initiate and run their own programs, but having someone experienced with deliberation and consensus-building can be a vital resource. One who does not talk down to people but keeps the environment safe for playfully questioning our assumptions and rearticulating them, eventually coming to "understand the particularities of the local situation, the terms, and the reference points of local identities." (Taylor 2020, p.21) Such facilitators need the sensitivity to notice the local differences and the skills to articulate these. The point is not for them to make the right decisions all themselves, but to ensure the right decisions get made with everyone's input.

Scattered throughout the population we need people to take upon themselves the personal responsibility for serving and helping others by just listening and facilitating discussion. This takes more than just tolerance it takes looking at things from all sides, actually listening to others and explaining one's point of view while being willing to modify it in deliberation. This is the true meaning of respect and is a basic democratic virtue. The job is to often repeat and remind people of the 'mission statement'; the vision toward which we are striving and the values by which we are to get there, occasionally updating words to be more perceptive and resonate more deeply.

*

Before we diagnose what is wrong with today's culture we need to understand what it is to get social or civic virtues right. I begin by looking at Reliabilism and Responsibilism in virtue epistemology, how our intellectual or moral virtues affect the way we are able to obtain the truth, and how we develop these different virtues. Examples of each are 'emotional intelligence,' being aware of the differences in oneself and others of feelings and motivations, *and* 'critical thinking,' examining things from all sides and being able to change one's mind in light of evidence. But what if the other won't reciprocate? How should we deal with misinformation? I canvas some preliminary strategies; the social media may police themselves through 'fact-checking' or being fined, terrorists can be jailed and cult-members deprogrammed. But maybe, just maybe, we might use educational campaigns to encourage deliberation among the citizens. This last move takes more than just tolerance, it takes actually listening to others and explaining one's point of view. Radical! It used to be that conservatives, liberals, and socialists agreed on creating the welfare state and only disagreed on how to get there and what that meant. That was after they had defeated fascism. The promise to the WWII veterans was they would inherit a better world, and they did for a while. Now, not only do we disagree on spin or policy, but we disagree about reality itself, with the result that fascist tendencies are on the rise again.

B) Virtue Epistemology:

Reliabilism and Responsibilism

A kind person knows what it is like to be confronted with a requirement of kindness. The sensitivity is, we might say, a sort of perceptual capacity. (McDowell 2002, p. 51)

Occasion by occasion, one knows what to do, not by applying universal principles but by being a certain kind of person. (McDowell 2002, p.73)

Virtue epistemology is when the characterization of knowledge is displaced from the nature of the proposition known to the person having the knowledge. Do they have the right credentials to claim knowledge? S is justified in believing p, rather than S's belief in p is justified. There are two schools of thought in virtue epistemology: Reliabilism and Responsibilism. These roughly correspond to the qualities of Aristotle's intellectual and moral virtues. Reliable intellectual virtues can operate accurately with little to no conscious control, like acute perception, logic, or empathy. Moral virtues, which we are responsible for developing and refining over time, help when good belief is produced by good believers; being meticulous is good, carelessness is bad. The former kind of virtues reflect our faculties; the latter reflects our person.

Reliabilism/Emotional Intelligence

Reliabilism holds true belief to be produced and retained by reliable truth-conducive cognitive faculties or competent powers and abilities in certain domains under normal circumstances, like accurate empathy. What makes knowledge valid for us is that we can reliably have the accurate perceptions or intellectual acumen needed to have that knowledge, such as using logic or having sympathy. Something more is required for true belief than mere justification; true belief must be *because of* or *attributable to* the knower's exercise of intellectual virtue. Knowledge is a kind of success from an ability that is an achievement manifesting the intellectual virtue of the believer, this falls short when it is merely true belief or

226

dumb luck. (Greco and Reibsamen 2018, p.725-731) The most common examples of reliable knowledge virtues are perceptual which are often automatic and can be conclusively proven true or false, right or wrong by how well it hits its intended target - the truth.

The virtue of 'emotional intelligence' (Seligman 2002, p.143-4) involves being accurately aware of the differences in oneself and among others of feelings, moods, temperaments, motivations, and intentions. This insight also has to reliably result in right action, and so further divides into the social and personal. Social intelligence is not just introspection or psychology, but has to respond well with social skill. One has to get it right. Personal intelligence is the ability to use one's feelings to accurately understand one's motives and guide one's behaviour. The opposite of emotional intelligence is to be clueless, self-deceived, lacking insight.

It is not known how much these kinds of intelligences are genetic but it seems possible to support and develop them in a facilitating environment over time. Education in psychology with plenty of classroom discussions among vastly different students helps, especially using role playing to put oneself in the perspective of another, but the child has to be well raised and nurtured before going to school.

> Part of what the parent tries to do is to bring the child to see the particular circumstances that here and now make certain emotions appropriate. The parent helps the child to compose the scene in the right way. This will involve persuading the child that the situation at hand is to be construed in this way rather than that, that what the child took to be a deliberate assault and cause for anger was really only an accident, that the laughter and smiles which annoy were intended as signs of delight rather than of teasing, that a particular distribution, though painful to endure, is in fact fair – that if one looked at the situation from the point of view of others involved, one would come to that conclusion. (Sherman 1999, p.242)

Initially we're forced to take a leap of faith on a strategy, followed by an intense emotional reaction to its consequences. This adds to the experience of the learner. After enough of these experiences we develop intuitions that shortcut deliberation. After enough practice in trying out alternative interpretations, testing and verifying them, the child will sharpen their perceptions, feelings, intuitions, and responses to be more spontaneously accurate and appropriate.

Responsibilism/Critical Thinking

Responsibilism says it matters what we do in rationally processing reliable input, such as having a fair and open mind in assessing contrary arguments, a style of thinking for which we are morally responsible and which improves with practice. It seeks to promote intellectual well-being, or wisdom and perspective. It sees intellectual virtues as good intellectual character traits, acquired habits of excellent thoughts and praiseworthy motivations. A belief formed or retained through epistemically praiseworthy affective-motivational states has some positive epistemic standing because of it. Such intellectual virtues reflect more the value of their possessor than on the reliability of their truth. Good belief is produced by good believers. To be pigheaded is to be blame-worthy. To be respectful is admirable.

This has implications for our democracy. We personally, as engaged citizens, need to exercise the intellectual virtue of 'critical thinking and judgement' defined by the *Character Strengths and Virtues* handbook as: "thinking things through and examining them from all sides; *not* jumping to conclusions; being able to change one's mind in light of evidence; weighing all evidence fairly." (Seligman and Peterson 2004, p.29) This takes more than just tolerance, it takes actually listening to others and explaining one's point of view while being willing to modify it in deliberation. Explaining one's reasoning is how we show respect, as well as actually listening. The opposite of being critically self-reflective is tribalism, myside bias, stereotyping, and inflexible dogmatism.

Education in philosophy which looks at the pros and cons of each side to an issue accompanied with plenty of classroom discussions among very different students helps but by itself it does not create an open mind, that takes personal initiative. Counter-information can heighten counter-arguing rather than updating. One may research the other side for ammunition to use; those who are more knowledgeable and reflective can be more prone to motivated reasoning. Those who go surfing the internet may come across new unexpected information that may affect their decisions, while those who are forced to watch information counter to their opinions may resent it and the end effect can be more polarizing. It is easier to say what impedes open-mindedness than what aids it. According to Seligman and Peterson (2004) this particular virtue of critical thinking is especially inhibited by three pervasive cognitive tendencies.

Virtue Realism

1. 'Selective exposure' is defined as maintaining one's
    beliefs by "exposing themselves to information that
    they already know is likely to support what they want
    to believe." (Seligman and Peterson 2004, p.154)
    Anthony Downs (1957) justifies it as cutting down on
    information costs. It is within the individual's choice to
    maximize what is useful to one's positions while
    minimizing the efforts of research.

2. 'Primacy effects' is when a tentative hypothesis
    becomes resistant to counterevidence. It seems "the
    evidence that comes first matters more" when the
    order shouldn't matter. This is why we should not
    jump to conclusions. One should sample different
    news channels to change the source of news from
    which they first come into contact covering a story. It is
    a matter of first impressions.

3. 'Polarization' is when you have mixed evidence and
    "people discount the evidence against their beliefs and
    then proceed to count the evidence on their side,

forgetting that it seems better only because they did not subject it to critical scrutiny." (Seligman and Peterson 2004, p.155) This is what happens in polemics when people are polarized against their opponents. It involves one's relationship to one's interpersonal environment.

Aristotle distinguished between the intellectual and moral virtues, but Reliabilism and Responsibilism are compatible. Virtue is both a sensitivity and a skill. In Virtues of the Mind (1996) Linda Zagzebski mixes Reliabilism with Responsibilism emphasizing the latter. She subsumes intellectual virtues under moral ones, except intellectual virtues have the singular underlying motivation to obtain the truth and avoid error. An act of intellectual virtue requires that one is successful in reaching the truth and is successful because one is acting and is motivated as would be the virtuous person. It cannot be by luck. The open-minded must reliably succeed at considering the views of others and reach a true belief as a result. It is a mixed theory because it requires both a characteristic internal motive (an emotion or feeling that initiates and directs action towards an end) and external success in achieving the virtue's end. In order to fulfill our intellectual cum moral responsibility we must rely on some reliable contact with reality. If someone finds they're wrong the virtuous person will change their epistemic patterns. We hold some responsibility for reliably getting it right. And a virtue's success depends on reliably accommodating the truth, which defines the necessary condition for something to even be an act of virtue. Jumping to hasty conclusions is not virtuous reasoning, wishful thinking is not acting on virtuous motivation. We need to be open to learning new information that can correct us.

C) Motivated Reasoning

What happens when we want to know the truth but it is at odds with our pre-existing belief system? Reverend Bayes said we should form a preference or make a decision by evaluating the evidence independent of the desired conclusion. However, people have a tendency to engage in 'motivated reasoning' when there is a confirmation bias to favor information congruent with prior attitudes, and/or a disconfirmation bias to deny, denigrate and counter-argue evidence that does not support us. Both of these, individually and together, further partisanship and extremism. (Cotter, Lodge, Vidigal 2020) When presented with a political cue, pro and con emotional reactions hit us before we have a chance to think about them. We have to overcome our lightning fast responses through deliberation or sober second thought, and when it is called for we must be able to either relax or change the prior positions we hold in our long term memories. According to Seligman and Peterson (2004) the vices that undermine critical thinking and open-mindedness are the selective exposure resulting from individual choices and the polarization of the us versus them in the social environment. These are the internal and external causes of extremism.

Selective Exposure

In *An Economic Theory of Democracy* (1957) the neoliberal Public Choice theorist Anthony Downs said it is true democracy works best when everyone is fully informed, but it is not rational for everyone to be equally informed. There is a cost to gathering information such as the opportunity cost of foregone alternatives, or the time and effort spent in assimilating data and weighing alternatives. Our news-sources should focus our attention on facts germane to making a decision, broad enough to report anything significant but narrow enough to edit out anything useless. From all the data available we must select the information most relevant. Any standard is biased and all selection is evaluative. There is no such thing as purely objective reporting.

To cut information costs voters listen to friends, those they know whose opinions they respect, or read subsidized literature like newspapers in the library. A problem with subsidized material is it is more likely to reflect the views of sponsors than one's own. We should read those whose principles of selection are the most like ours, the only difference being they have more information we could use. We come to our selection principles through trial and error, following those evaluations that have led most consistently to our cherished objectives. Then we compare different media to see how close they remain to our perspective.

According to Downs we continue seeking information until marginal return equals marginal cost, with an assumption of decreasing returns from the knowledge sought and the increasing costs of obtaining even more. Investment is determined by the importance of making a right decision multiplied by the probability that a new detail will affect one's decision. A voter only needs the information that will affect their vote. Those already decided need no new information, and those who don't care can use it but are not inclined to get it. The value of one's vote depends on the importance of getting it right, but a single vote makes little difference. Downs scandalized people when he said if someone was rational they wouldn't vote.

This is an account of what we would normally do, which can be criticized as not what we should do. There is a normative side to knowledge such that it can't be naturalized. It is idealized rational acceptability and able to critique anything put in its place. Maybe we should listen to contrasting opinions since we can never know beforehand what will change our mind. Maybe we need to understand the other point of view in order to better live with our fellow citizens. If we only listen to whoever agrees with us, we can be cut off from the rest of the world. Assuming there is no such thing as objective reporting, one will not try to find balance. We cut down costs by listening to those we trust, but this can be like an echo chamber bringing our messages back to us with no disconfirming counterevidence that can correct us. Fideism, the idea that one can simply believe on faith alone, makes it seem like a personal choice to decide for oneself what is true or not while ignoring any contrary claims. This attacks the intellectual integrity that feels the need to actually be right regardless of what one may want that to be. To change our mind if we find we're wrong. We may have to rely on our strongest intuitions, but these have to be tested. We have to be willing to question ourselves. We cannot tell before hand what will change our mind and our understanding can be infinitely corrected and refined.

Polarization

Downs thought there should be a single peaked preference curve for the overall ideological tastes of voters, and political parties ranged in general around the center or most popular part of the electorate. This was in 1957, at the height of the cold war, when policies for the separate ideologies were too alike to tell much of a difference between the parties. The worst case scenario for him is when there is a valley, opposites in a civil war between ideological extremes with little common ground, such as we see in America today. One side stonewalls, while blaming the partisanship of the other side for nothing getting done thereby creating a false equivalency. Also, we may not be willing to give an inch or admit we may be wrong if the opposition will gleefully gloat over pouncing on any sign of weakness. Now each side has their own news channels claiming the other is 'fake news.' Narrowcasting is where a media outlet seeks only a small slice of the audience rather than addressing as many people as possible. This has been coupled with on-line search engines that track what gets our attention in order to find news items that would interest us, and with which we are already likely to agree. The result is echo chambers within social media, blogs, talk radio and podcasts, and cable television communities.

Problem is such isolated information silos can lead to tribalism, where true believers may come to persecute heretics. Polemics is the most extreme of intellectual abuse. In polemics, the polemicist assumes upon himself ...

> rights authorizing him to wage war and making that struggle a just undertaking; the person he confronts is not a partner in the search for truth, but an adversary, an enemy who is wrong, who is harmful and whose very existence constitutes a threat. ... [T]he game does not consist of recognizing this person as a subject having the right to speak, but of abolishing him, as interlocutor, from any possible dialogue. (Foucault 1984 p.381-3)

For Foucault (1984) the pleasant but difficult game of 'reciprocal elucidation' was the alternative to polemics. The rights and duties of each person are immanent to the dialogue. The questioner has the right "to remain unconvinced, to perceive a contradiction, to require more information, to emphasize different postulates, to point out faulty reasoning, etc." (Foucault 1984 p.381) The one answering is tied to what they have said earlier and the questioning of the other. This give-and-take affects our relationship both to the truth and to each other. Foucault did a lot of interviews.

In a situation like the US the intellectual virtue of an open and fair mind is even more important to cultivate. Partisanship is tribal and creates what Irving Janis (1982) calls 'groupthink' which falls into error through myside bias (his example was the Cuban missile crisis), he thought someone should play devil's advocate to make sure the other side is heard and considered. Since the first step in statistics is the null hypothesis, which tries to prove there is no correlation to be tested. Unfortunately, this can come across as too antagonistic. One has to be careful and courteous, which takes emotional/social sensitivity. An open mind does not mean one cannot have preferences, but one should not do so without understanding the alternatives and testing one's beliefs. This is what *should* happen.

Defining the Problem

But what do you do when the other won't reciprocate and continues to spew divisive rhetoric? What if people put tribalism before the truth? If information is cynically seen as merely serving the interests of those who invest in it, then it may just as well produce ignorance. There are those whose professional job is to manufacture doubt by portraying falsehoods as truths. An effective delaying tactic used by cigarette companies avoiding class-action lawsuits was telling contrary claims that look exactly the same as scientific publications, so people were left thinking the experts disagreed, which they don't (Michaels

2008). This tactic has been used against attempts to combat the global warming that results in climate change. The offending companies don't even have to actually prove their side's point; they just have to raise enough reasonable doubt to delay judgement, hopefully indefinitely (Oreskes and Conway 2010).

This has dire consequences for our knowledge. The American tradition of fundamentalist fideism, belief based on faith alone, makes it seem a personal right to be up to individuals themselves to freely choose what is true and ignore any contrary claims. But, this is the opposite of rational deliberation. There is a difference between questions calling for expert scientific knowledge and those calling for ethics or common opinion. Fideism attacks science and replaces it with spin, ranging from creationism to conspiracy theories. Danger is when true believers try to root out heretics. This can happen when people moralize differences of opinions. Add to this apocalyptic fears about the decline of civilization rationalizing any possible violence. According to David Barker and Morgan Marietta (2020) there are three consequences from fighting over alternative realities.

1. Dueling fact perceptions can cause social contempt and alienation; if someone sees a co-worker spouting 'misinformation' from the right or 'fake news' from the left they may refuse to work with them, a reaction worse than mere partisanship.

2. The result of extreme polarization over the truth is policy gridlock; if democratic decision-makers cannot agree on the facts, productive debate is impossible. Uncertainty resulting from obstruction or inconsistency between governments can threaten the markets and foreign policies.

3. And, accountability is also impossible; a president can commit a crime and get away with it because their followers deny any such crime took place. Poor performance becomes irrelevant and scandals become toothless.

Virtue Realism

How are we to respond to the fanatically blind consumption of misinformation? The most extreme response is 'deprogramming' a brainwashed member of a cult. This was popular during the Seventies and is still used in counter-espionage. First you begin by discrediting the figure of authority, the cult leader. Presenting the target with contradictions (ideology versus reality) until they begin to listen. As reality takes precedence over ideology the subject can begin to open up and voice resentments against the cult. Finally, they can then come to identify with the deprogrammer and against the former cult. The problem is deprogramming is manipulative and does not properly respect freewill, such as in kidnapping. It uses force and possibly violence.

In respecting the individual consumer's freedom, should we take a legal course instead and hold responsible those who manufacture misinformation, making social-media accountable; liable for slander, lying, and misleading information? For example, Smartmatic is suing, to the tune of $2.7 Billion damages for defamation, the Fox News personalities Maria Bartiromo, Lou Dobbs and Jeanine Pirro, as well as attorneys Rudy Giuliani and Sidney Powell for spreading the Big Lie of voter fraud due to their voting machines. Dominion Voting is suing Fox News for $1.6 Billion for the same reason. They claim the channel "recklessly disregarded the truth" because "the lies were good for Fox's business."

Problem is to prevent misinformation in the future it would have to be policed and prosecuted, which runs counter to the right of free speech and freedom of the press. But the original justification for free speech was that truth will be found and errors uncovered when exposed to the light of day. Now, there are those whose professional job is to manufacture doubt by portraying falsehoods as truths. Fox News looks like every other news channel and has some good integral journalists, like Chris Wallace. Yet with the opinions aired on some shows everyone is supposed to be in on the joke, but people *do* take them seriously. Wikipedia states that:

> In September 2020, a federal judge, in dismissing a defamation lawsuit regarding statements Carlson made on Tucker Carlson Tonight, cited her acceptance of Fox News' defense that, given that the "general tenor" of the show is to "challenge political correctness and media bias," Carlson is not "stating actual facts" on its show, but instead employs "exaggeration" and "non-literal commentary". The judge also agreed with Fox News' defense that reasonable viewers would have "skepticism" over statements Carlson makes on its show.

But people still *do* take him seriously and rank him as more credible than more traditional cable news hosts. Some have even suggested he could make a presidential hopeful. 'Infotainment' is ambiguous between journalistic information and political entertainment; it can be hard to tell the difference when one blends into the other. In the end it may not matter anyway, radicals can plausibly deny they are responsible for any violent consequences from their angry partisan rhetoric, since if they didn't tell the audience to do exactly what they actually did, it would fail the Brandenburg test and they won't be held accountable. Besides, many politicians are too afraid of their base to correct them. And those who spread divisive paranoid conspiracy theories can defend themselves by saying they're only asking questions, leaving it up to the audience to ponder. If we do not take the threat of misleading misinformation seriously, we will not protect ourselves from it. This *is* the problem.

But what can we do? Any 'fact checking' the social-media does perform on themselves can fail to reach the intended audience and then merely gets dismissed as 'wrong!' by the increasingly resistant believer; the problem is to sell advertising the algorithms of social-media seek to prolong the viewer's attention and end up using fear and outrage to do so, which is divisive in itself. On the other hand, terrorism and hate speech are obviously serious criminal offenses that should be prosecuted. Between the extremes of self-policing and criminal sanctions, we tend to use fines to influence patterns of transgression.

The Neoliberal Answer

Fines are an integral part of the legal environment enabling markets to function. Gary Becker (1968/1976) saw a diminishing marginal utility to exterminating crime. The question became how much crime can we tolerate? The way to correct errors is to make the fines and sentences too expensive to ignore, not probe into a subject's psychology in trying to eliminate deviance down to the smallest detail. No need for an authority to micromanage the subject, just make a surface adjustment in the environment and let the effects work themselves out.

A simple adjustment in economic policies can affect free market behaviour, without relying on regulations and quotas determined by out-of-touch central committees. A spontaneous order has more complexity than a deliberate arrangement. The details are too complicated for a central authority to understand and use properly. The government should be limited to enforcing those universal rules which will enable spontaneous order. Laws can create an economy that regulates itself. Such laws will be abstract and without full concrete detail. Friederich Hayek (1967) thought laws should intervene in a way that is purely general, not tied to a specific purpose. It should be the rules of the game, whose outcome is not predetermined by the arbitrary will of authorities and committees. He favored only the negative liberty from interference, violence, theft, and fraud as well as the disallowance of laws that can't be properly universalized, as Kant had said. The rule of law is not a command legitimately ordered but one equally applicable to all. It is not the source of power but the limitation of power that prevents arbitrary coercion. Those who govern best govern less.

'Law and economics' is one of the new right-wing academic subjects inspired by Hayek. He thought laws make markets possible and define them, they are not given as something natural. That means we are not stuck with a capitalism that has its own internal logic but can invent a new one. The question becomes how to modify the material, cultural, technical, and legal basis to promote markets where they don't already exist.

Hayek (1945) thought the market is a superior information processor, so instead of special interests maybe *it* should allocate the funding for research in a free market of ideas. He organized the conference that created the Mont Pelerin Society on April 10th, 1947. This is an international organization of think tanks for generating policy talking points for friendly politicians. Members originally included Karl Popper, Ludwig von Mises, Milton Friedman and eventually Gary Becker. Membership is still by invitation only. Karl Popper thought socialists should be invited to test the group's assumptions, he understood the first step of an experiment is to test the null hypothesis where one tries to prove there is no correlation to be tested. Such was the ideal of Popper's 'open society.' The Austrian Libertarian Ludwig von Mises would have none of it, no way he was going to allow in socialists! Hayek wanted the Mont Pelerin Society to supersede the socialist Fabian Society; an ideological alternative that replaces the latter and improves on the international functioning of think tanks.

The result has been echo-chambers that multiply broadcast the same messages from different outlets run by some of the same people. As Philip Mirowski explained about the Mont Pelerin Society, the loose coupling of their organizations makes conspiracy deniable.

> I will use the term "thought collective" to refer to
> this multilevel, multiphase, multisector approach
> to the building of political capacity to incubate,

> critique, and promulgate ideas. ... Outsiders would rarely perceive the extent to which individual protagonists embedded in a particular shell served multiple roles, or the strength and pervasiveness of network ties, since they could never see beyond the immediate shell doll right before their noses. ... The Russian doll structure of the Neoliberal Thought collective would tend to amplify and distribute the voice of any one member throughout a series of seemingly different organizations, personas, and broadcast settings, lending it resonance and gravitas, not to mention fronting an echo chamber for ideas right at the time when hearing them was most propitious. (Mirowski, 2013, p. 43 & 46 & 49)

Mirowski argues that concentric from the MPS, which is international, are the academic departments dominated by neoliberal intellectuals, the foundations that fund conservative research, think tanks with quick and timely talking-points for friendly politicians, and talking heads for television news shows and opinion periodicals to show and convince the end-consumers. With many of the same people filling dissimilar roles, though loosely coupled it acts as a fairly tight network partitioning off opposition. It's an echo-chamber enclosed upon itself that can further pull us into extremism.

There is another effect the Society has had upon knowledge and the information environment. According to Philip Mirowski the Mont Pelerin Society has also adopted neoconservative Leo Strauss' double standard of truth. Esoteric secrets for the wise few and exoteric doctrine for the masses.

> Neoliberals preach that the market is the unforgiving arbiter of all political action; but they absolve themselves from its rule. They propound libertarian freedoms but practice the most regimented hierarchy in their political organization; they sermonize about spontaneous order, while plotting to take over the state; they catechize prostration of the self before the awesome power of the knowledge conveyed by the market, but issue themselves sweeping dispensations. (Mirowski, 2013, pp. 98-99)

Virtue Realism

They see the free market as the ultimate site of truth for everyone but themselves. Neoliberalism seems to be at first sight a levelling doctrine that disparages elites and affirms the wisdom of crowds. But spontaneous order applies to everyone but themselves; they quite intentionally intervene when it is to their interests, like creating the Mont Pelerin Society with its international network of think tanks. They were already ready waiting with policy advice for when the Keynesian hegemony toppled. They went against the prevailing market and succeeded. However, a double standard of truth is corrupt and can rot our institutions from within. People may say they believe in the right standards/ideals and act accordingly, but those who "know" better will see it all as just political posturing for social control.

Ultimately, the problem with corporate financing is it can come with strings attached, and the research can seem trivial such as the yellowing of paper. Corporate information is copy written and may not be freely shared.

Those with money or power may not like what a professional expert honestly has to say, especially if it is the truth and has disastrous implications. They may simply stop funding, eliminating any trace of a line of research without leaving anyone accountable. Meanwhile, any "paid" intellectual left over can be suspiciously dismissed as merely a mercenary apologist. The mere appearance of a conflict of interests looks bad and should be avoided at all cost. But if knowledge is to serve those who invest in it then it may just as well produce misinformation as not, which *is* what has to be fined. Those with deep enough pockets may ruthlessly look at any steep fines as simply the cost of doing business, especially if their half-truths have a large audience and makes lots of money, or supports desired policies. Can setting up the formal conditions of economic structures and leaving the rest up to the free market really be enough?

In the end there may be little the media itself can change anyway that would affect polarization except perhaps making it worse, since it may actually originate within an individual's selective attention. People have to be inspired to initiate open-mindedness and critical thinking in themselves. How do we inculcate the needed virtues? Perhaps by exercising the 'epistemic justice' of listening to and making allowances for alternative views, needed so much for a true and honest deliberation amongst one's peers. The more this is done in the environment the more it can facilitate others to be more able to do the same.

D) Virtue Epistemology Revisited in Deliberative Democracy

Habermas (1996) had written that "reporting facts as human-interest stories, mixing information with entertainment, arranging material episodically, and breaking down complex relationships into smaller fragments" in dumbing down the audience is supposed to depoliticize public communications, but with the media today even wearing protective gear has been politicized. This animus is not just the result of introducing comprehensive doctrines into public reasoning, as Rawls would interpret it, but the partisan spread of fake news and misinformation itself which is worse.

Both philosophers were against holding a highly partisan division that only cares about their own side winning. Rawls argued we need to respect the duty of civility which means listening to the other side and adjusting our position if needed, as well as respecting reciprocity by putting forth claims we sincerely think the other can accept, but he did not include the mass media in public reason because there was no interactive dialogue. Habermas was against having rigid highly partisan positions where communication was replaced by transactional bribes and threats that cared more about outcomes than the truth. He called this strategic as opposed to communicative action.

Virtue Realism

Neither asked what happens when lies have democratic success with consequences, and what can protect us then? They were constructivists not realists. A democracy was supposed to winnow out misinformation. They dealt with the undue influence of wealth and power, but not intentionally broadcasting lies and having people believe them, except to say we all need a decent education in processing and weighing evidence. This means properly funding public education.

In order to see what else we might need, we return back to Reliabilism and Responsibilism as the different kinds of epistemological virtues to be desired. According to the 'Reliabilist Virtue Epistemology' of John Greco and Jonathan Reibsamen (2018, p.734-737) testimonials, such as asking a stranger for directions, depend on someone else for their truth. But whether or not someone's belief-forming disposition is an intellectual virtue still depends on external facts. Some social environments enable us to trust the word of others, some not. To trust those who seem trustworthy is an intellectual virtue in the former not the latter. Knowing who to trust can never be reliable for the individual in the latter case because of the social context. The virtue by itself cannot be reliable because of social epistemic dependence. Yet, the disposition to trust another's word is still the individual's; one can have a variety of social cognitive virtues that enables one to navigate the social world. How important is the contribution of a hearer's abilities to count as knowledge? Our cognitive abilities must contribute in the right way, according to the various needs of those in dialogue, to the reliable production of true belief. Can we accurately feel and understand the other's intentions and motives, responding accordingly with understanding, respect, and fairness?[9]

---

[9] This sensitivity and grace is much more needed than the intellectual courage of speaking truth to power or persevering against the grain of conformity, favoured so much by the 'creative-genius' understanding of the scientific/artistic tradition, which can calcify opposition.

Virtue Realism

How do we properly develop reliable social cognitive abilities? The 'virtue responsibilist epistemology' of Miranda Fricker's *Epistemic Injustice* (2007) combines the moral concern of social justice with that of knowledge, making knowledge itself a moral concern we ourselves are responsible for fostering. Testimonial injustice is where someone is granted low credibility because they belong to a stigmatized group. This does not have to affect us at the level of beliefs because the social imagination can already be influencing us below the conscious level through the subtlety of our feelings. Therefore, it is below the threshold of the ideal speech situation for Habermas. Fricker believes injustice is more a baseline and justice an accomplishment. We need to become self aware of how we may be perceiving people in an epistemically prejudicial light and compensate in how we consider their testimonies. 'Fairness' as defined by Seligman and Peterson (2004, p.392) holds everyone deserves respect whether you personally like them or not, they should be treated with dignity and given a chance to prove themselves.

Deliberative democracy can be a great equalizer in being free and inclusive, while trying to eliminate manipulation and coercion. Stephen Elstub (2018) explains that in deliberation everyone, even elites, have to justify their demands. It is thus harder to promote self-interest, enabling subordinate groups to highlight why inequalities are wrong. Youth, minorities, and those with lower incomes are more willing to deliberate and the actual participation in deliberation is less biased and skewed than with voting. Francesca Poletta and Beth Gharrity Gardner (2018) argue that women, minorities, and the poor are more likely to deliberate by telling emotionally touching stories of their personal history and how they have been impacted by an issue, they are generally not educated experts talking in the abstract universal detached logic favoured by policy-making discourse. Instead, their casual discourse helps inform us about the true nature of our preferences by bringing out how we stand in relation to options or consequences we have never before considered, and exercises our empathy in making allowances for other perspectives.

Alternatively, Fricker's 'epistemic injustice' hurts the hearer because one may miss important information through bias, and harms the speaker because it robs them of an opportunity to develop their abilities to testify insofar as they never get asked *and* to see their testimony valued as a collaborative informant not just an objectified source of information. Epistemic justice on the other hand benefits both the person who develops it and those with whom they interact; and is most effective at the level of social institutions.

Fricker does not include 'credibility excess' as an incident of epistemic injustice because it only harms the person receiving it when it is cumulative enough to lead to blind arrogance. I would say that credibility excess really hurts the one who commits the error and the best defence against it is to practice 'epistemic justice' by listening to other points of view. The answer is to practice more of the same virtue. Against Downs' idea that democracy is simply the selection of competing elites, deliberation functions best when it is public, inclusive, and egalitarian. For Elstub, 'legitimacy' requires the input and assent of all those affected by a decision and has to be based on considerations of all relevant reasons. Wright (2018, p.759) comments that uncovering intellectual vice can help us find where to improve and accusing someone of epistemic injustice is a deeper criticism of those with intractable (but coherent) sets of beliefs.

Unfortunately, being open-minded all by ourselves may simply allow the other side the chance to spread their disinformation. Each side wants the other to be open minded; to try and understand *their* point of view so they can possibly change the other's mind. Or at least not have them oppose us and get in our way. Open-mindedness takes personal initiative because it only benefits someone who honestly wants to find out the truth for themselves; someone who hasn't already made up their mind, since it doesn't guarantee any side's success. One must desire to know the truth no matter what that might be; we are supposed to put country before party. We are supposed to look for where we may be wrong, so we can learn and improve. (See appendix)

Appendix: Hegel's List of Rationalizations

In the *Elements of the Philosophy of Right* (1821/1991, II:139), Hegel argued that without us recognizing its authority, the Good is impotent and will not be actualized. It is true that our actions should be seen by us to be valid. However, because our actions take place in the world, we cannot do whatever we happen to feel like doing. When we let our will be determined by our drives and desires, this means we have not stepped back and prioritized our first order impulses or tested their worthiness. Questioning our impulses is our freedom and responsibility. It is not the naturalness of our inclinations, or turning into ourselves for guidance, that makes for evil but simply that what we may do should not be done. We are responsible for choosing evil over the good by letting our impulses take precedence over what is right.

Hegel (II:140, 1821/1991) offers a **complete** list of moral rationalizations for excusing wrongdoing. Most people rely on one of these. Which ones do you recognize in yourself and others? We need to find which one(s) we use, be aware of them and compensate for the flaw.

1.   Evil is where people know better but do what is wrong anyway. This can be because they are weak, or don't care whether something is right or wrong, they just want what they want and all that matters is getting their way. With the former, there is some hope they may eventually overcome their weakness. With the latter, talking is futile. Self-deception enters the picture when people believe the good is whatever they want it to be. In cases where we do not bother to test the validity of our actions, we are responsible for our own ignorance. If we do not know better, maybe we should.

2.   When accused of a wrong some people point to the good they do at other times to reveal examples of how their traits express the opposite quality. They do not realize they are inconsistent.

3.	Another excuse is to point out that even experts disagree, so we can take our pick of whatever philosophies may justify the course of action we want to take.

4.	Then, there is justification by good intentions. We may mean well, and we can put a positive spin upon any reason. Coupled with this is the idea that the ends justify the means, which can involve using something that is not supposed to be a means at all, thereby violating something sacrosanct. We can thus turn what is more important into a matter of opinion based on the feelings, imagination, and caprice of the individual.

5.	The intensity of our convictions may delude us into believing our conscience is securely certain of its truth. Having complete trust in our conscience we may not feel we need to test the validity of our desires. If we follow our conscience, it can be thought that while we may be mistaken, we are not culpable. However, in Hegel's time there was a student who was sure a certain writer was a saboteur. He may have been right. The student sincerely felt it was his patriotic duty to kill the traitor. The reaction against this crime was so strong, the student ended up doing more for the enemy's cause than the dead author ever could.

6.   The most corrupt philosophy is to believe that subjective opinion is our ultimate and final arbiter. This is the favorite rationalization for artists. Good and bad are held by this view to be a matter of refinement and taste. These people believe the individual gives things whatever value they have through the effort they put into them. The question becomes whether we can be as strong and determined as we need to be to create and forge new values or great 'works of art;' the 'beautiful soul' suffers from over-sensitivity. Aristotle truthfully said that in art those who broke the rules at will were often geniuses, while in morals those who broke the rules at will were criminals (NE 1140b22-5). These villains may still hope that the misunderstood and unappreciated artist may become vindicated after they are dead. But this is still a matter of dumb luck, and their impact may not be good.

Bibliography

Ackerman, B. (1984). Discovering the Constitution. *Yale Law Journal*, 93: 1013-72.

Ahuvia, Aaron and Izberk-Bilgin, Elif. (2013). Well-Being in Consumer Society. In S. A. David, *The Oxford Handbook of Happiness* (pp. 482-497). Oxford: Oxford UP.

Anderson, E. (1993). *Value in Ethics and Economics.* Cambridge: Harvard UP.

Arendt, H. (1958). *The Human Condition.* Chicago: U of C Press.

Arendt, H. (1963). The Revolutionary Tradition and Its Lost Treasure. In H. Arendt, *On Revolution* (pp. 207-273). NY: Penguin Books.

Aristotle. (2009). *Nicomachean Ethics.* (D. Ross, Trans.) N.Y., N.Y.: Oxford UP.

Arrow, K. (1951). *Social Choice and Individual Values.* London: Yale UP.

Barker, David and Merietta, Morgan. (2020). Misinformation, Fake News, and Dueling Fact Perceptions in Public Opinion and Elections. In E. Suhay, B. Grofman, & A. Treschel, *The Oxford Handbook of Electoral Persuasion* (pp. 493-522). Oxford: Oxford UP.

Becker, G. (1976). Crime and Punishment: An Economic Approach. In G. Becker, *The Economic Approach to Human Behaviour* (pp. 39-85). Chicago: U of Chicago Press.

Bessette, J. (1980). Deliberative Democracy: The Majority Principle in Republican Government. In R. Goldwin, & W. Schambra, *How Democratic is the Constitution?* (pp. 102-116). Washington: AEI.

Black, D. (1958). *The Theory of Committees and Elections.* Cambridge: Cambridge UP.

Bibliography

Brink, D. (1989). *Moral Realism and the Foundations of Ethics*. Cambridge: Cambridge UP.

Buchanan, James M. and Tullock, Gordon. (1962). *The Calculus of Consent: Logical Foundations of Constitutional Democracy*. Indianapolis: Liberty Fund.

Cahoone, L. (2010b). *The Modern Intellectual Tradition: From Descartes to Derrida - Lectures 19-36*. Chantilly: The Great Courses.

Cohen, J. (1989/1997). Deliberation and Democratic Legitimacy. In J. Bohman, & W. Rehg, *Deliberative Democracy* (pp. 67-87). Cambridge: MIT Press.

Cotter, Ryan Milton Lodge and Robert Vidigal. (2020). When, How, and Why Persuasion Fails: A Motivated Reasoning Account. In E. Suhay, B. Grofman, & A. H. Trechsel, *Oxford Handbook of Electoral Persuasion* (pp. 51-65). Oxford: Oxford UP.

Dancy, J. (2004). *Ethics Without Principles*. Oxford:
Clarendon Press.

Dancy, J. (2006). Nonnaturalism. In D. Copp, *The Oxford
Handbook of Ethical Theory* (pp. 122-145). Osford:
Oxford UP.

Dewey, J. (1927). *The Public and its Problems*. Athens:
Swallow Press.

Downs, A. (1957). *An Economic Theory of Democracy*. NY:
Harper & Row.

Dray, W. H. (1993). *Philosophy of History*. N.J.: Prentice-
Hall Inc.

Elster, J. (1986/1997). The Market and The Forum: Three
Varieties of Political Theory. In J. Bohman, & W.
Rehg, *Deliberative Democracy* (pp. 3-34).
Cambridge: MIT Press.

Elstub, S. (2018). Deliberative and Participatory
Democracy. In A. Bachtiger, J. S. Dryzeck, J.

Mansbridge, & M. E. Warren, *The Oxford Handbook of Deliberative Democracy* (pp. 187-202). Oxford: Oxford UP.

Floridia, A. (2017). *From Participation to Deliberation: A Critical Genealogy of Deliberative Democracy.* Colchester: ecpr press.

Floridia, A. (2018). The Origins of the Deliberative Turn. In A. Bachtiger, J. S. Dryzeck, J. Mansbridge, & M. E. Warren, *The Oxford Handbook of Deliberative Democracy* (pp. 35-54). Oxford: Oxford UP.

Foucault, M. (1978/2008). *Security, Territory, Population.* NY: Picador.

Foucault, M. (1984). Polemics, Politics, and Problematizations. In M. Foucault, *The Foucault Reader* (pp. 381-390). NY: Vintage.

Foucault, M. (2008). *The Birth of Biopolitics: Lectures at the College de France 1978-1979.* NY: Picador.

Fricker, M. (2007). *Epistemic Injustice: Power and the Ethics of Knowing.* Oxford: Oxford UP.

Greco, J. a. (2018). Reliabilist Virtue Epistemology. In N. Snow, *The Oxford Handbook of Virtue* (pp. 725-746). Oxford: Oxford UP.

Habermas, J. (1983). Discourse Ethics: Notes on a Program of Philosophical Justification. In J. Habermas, *Moral Consciousness and Communicative Action* (pp. 43-115). Cambridge: MIT Press.

Habermas, J. (1988/1996). Popular Sovereignty as Procedure. In J. Habermas, *Between Facts and Norms: Contributions to a Discourse Theory of Law and Democracy* (pp. 463-490). Cambridge: MIT Press.

Habermas, J. (1992/1996). *Between Facts and Norms: Contributions to a Discourse Theory of Law and Democracy.* Cambridge: MIT Press.

Bibliography

Hayek, F. (1945). The Use of Knowledge in Society. *Library of Economics and Liberty.*

Hayek, F. (1967). Principles of a Liberal Social Order. In F. Hayek, *Studies in Philosophy, Politics, and Economics.* Chicago: University of Chicago Press.

Hegel, G. W. (1821/1991). *Elements of the Philosophy of Right.* (H. B. Nisbet, Trans.) Cambridge: Cambridge UP.

Janis, I. (1982). *Groupthink: Psychological studies of policy decisions and fiascos.* Boston: Houghton Mifflin.

Kuhn, T. (1962). *The Structure of Scientific Revolutions.* Chicago: U of C Press.

MacIntyre, A. (1981). *After Virtue.* Notre Dame: University of Notre Dame Press.

Manin, B. (1987). On Legitimacy and Political Deliberation. *Political Theory,* v. 15 n. 3, 338-368.

Mansbridge, J. (1980). *Beyond Adversary Democracy*. Chicago: Chicago UP.

McDowell, J. W. (2002). Virtue and Reason. In J. W. McDowell, *Mind, Value, & Reality* (pp. 50-73). Cambridge: Harvard UP.

Michaels, D. (2008). *Doubt is Their Product: How Industry's Assault on Science Threatens Your Health*. Oxford: Oxford UP.

Michelman, F. (1986). Forward: Traces of Self-government. *Harvard Law Review*, 100: 4-77.

Michelman, F. (1988). Law's Republic. *Yale Law Journal*, 98: 1493-537.

Mirowski, P. (2013). *Never Let a Serious Crisis Go to Waste: How Neoliberalism Survived the Financial Meltdown*. N.Y., N.Y.: Verso.

Moore, G. E. (1903). *Principia Ethica*. Cambridge: Cambridge UP.

Bibliography

Olson, M. (1965). *The Logic of Collective Action: Public Goods and the Theory of Groups.* Cambridge: Harvard UP.

Oreskes, Naomi and Conway, Erik M. (2010). *Merchants of Doubt: How a Handful of Scientists Obscured the Truth on Issues from Tobacco Smoke to Global Warming.* NY: Bloomsbury.

Pettit, P. (1997). *Republicanism: A Theory of Freedom and Government.* Oxford: Oxford UP.

Pocock, J. G. (1975). *The Machiavellian Moment: Florintine Political Thought and the Atlantic Republican Tradition.* Princeton: Princeton UP.

Polletta, Frecesca and Gardner, Beth Gharrity. (2018). The Forms of Deliberative Communication. In A. Bachtiger, J. S. Dryzeck, J. Mansbridge, & M. E. Warren, *The Oxford Handbook of Deliberative Democracy* (pp. 70-85). Oxford: Oxford UP.

Rawls, J. (1971). *A Theory of Justice.* MA: Harvard UP.

Rawls, J. (1980/1997). Kantian Constructivism in Moral
Theory. In S. Darwall, A. Gibbard, & P. Railton,
*Moral Discourse and Practice: Some Philosophical
Approaches* (pp. 247-266). Oxford: Oxford UP.

Rawls, J. (1993). *Political Liberalism.* NY: Columbia UP.

Rawls, J. (1997/2005). The Idea of Public Reason Revisited.
In J. Rawls, *Political Liberalism* (pp. 440-490). NY:
Columbia UP.

Riker, W. H. (1962). *The Theory of Political Coalitions.*
Westport: Greenwood Press.

Russell, D. C. (2009). *Practical Intelligence and the Virtues.*
Oxford: Oxford UP.

Sayers, D. (2002). Why Work? In E. Heath, *Morality and
the Market: Ethics & Virtue in the Conduct of
Business* (pp. 431-435). NY: McGraw Hill.

Bibliography

Seligman, M. (2002). *Authentic Happiness.* NY: Atria.

Seligman, Martin E P and Peterson, Christopher. (2004). *Character Strengths and Virtues: A Handbook and Classification.* Oxford: Oxford UP.

Sherman, N. (1999). The Habituation of Character. In N. Sherman, *Aristotle's Ethics: Critical Essays* (pp. 231-276). Lanham: Rowman and Littlefield.

Skinner, Q. (1984/2002). The idea of negative liberty: Machiavellian and modern perspectives. In Q. Skinner, *Visions of Politics Volume 2: Renaissance Virtues* (pp. 186-212). Cambridge: Cambridge UP.

Sunstein, C. (1984). Naked Preferences and the Constitution. *Columbia Law Review*, p.1689-1732.

Sunstein, C. (1985). Interest Groups in American Public Law. *Stanford Law Review*, p.29-87.

Sunstein, C. (1988). Beyond the Republican Revival. *Yale Law Journal*, p.1539-1590.

Taylor, C. (1989). *Sources of the Self: The Making of the Modern Identity.* Cambridge: Harvard UP.

Taylor, C. (1995). Coss-Purposes: The Liberal-Communitarian Debate. In C. Taylor, *Philosophical Arguments* (pp. 181-203). Cambridge: Harvard UP.

Taylor, C. (2020). *Reconstructing Democracy: How Citizens Are Building from the Ground Up.* Harvard: Harvard UP.

Tullock, G. (1965). *The Politics of Bureaucracy.* Indianapolis: Liberty Fund.

Wolff, R. P. (1968). *The Poverty of Liberalism.* Boston: Harvard UP.

Wright, S. (2018). Virtue Responsibilism. In N. Snow, *The Oxford Handbook of Virtue* (pp. 747-764). Oxford: Oxford UP.

Bibliography

Zagzebski, L. (1996). *Virtues of the Mind: An Inquiry into the Nature of Virtue and the Ethical Foundations of Knowledge.* Cambridge: Cambridge UP.

Zagzebski, L. (2017). *Exemplarist Moral Theory.* Oxford: Oxford UP.

9 798598 201695